CW00688321

TOUR OF THE MATTERHORN

About the Author

Hilary Sharp is British, a qualified Accompagnateur en Montagne (Trekking Guide), and is based permanently in the village of Vallorcine near Chamonix Mont Blanc in the French Alps. She runs her own trekking business, Trekking in the Alps, guiding walks in winter, spring and summer (info@trekkinginthealps. com; www.trekkinginthealps.com). Her love of walking and climbing has taken her to many parts of Europe and further afield.

Hilary contributes to several British walking magazines and is author *of Trekking and Climbing in the Western Alps* (New Holland, 2002).

Other Cicerone guidebooks by Hilary Sharp
Snowshoeing: Mont Blanc and the Western Alps
Mont Blanc Walks
Tour of Monte Rosa

TOUR OF THE MATTERHORN

by

Hilary Sharp

© Hilary Sharp 2006
Reprinted 2009 (with updates)
ISBN -10: 1 85284 472 8
ISBN-13: 978 1 85284 472 1
Maps: Jon de Montjoye
Photographs: Hilary Sharp and Jon de Montjoye

A catalogue record for this book is available from the British Library.

Acknowledgements

I would like to thank everyone who has walked this route with me, and especially those who have allowed me to photograph them; also the hut guardians and hoteliers who have welcomed me and shared their vast local knowledge with me. Information was also provided by Jean-Luc Lugon, Loredana and Silvia from Aosta. I would like to thank Jonathan Williams from Cicerone for saying 'Yes' (and for then being patient!), and most of all my husband, Jon de Montjoye, who drew the maps, walked some of the route with me, and once again had to live with me whilst I got to grips with the project.

Advice to Readers

Readers are advised that while every effort is taken by the author to ensure the accuracy of this guidebook, changes can occur which may affect the contents. It is advisable to check locally on transport, accommodation, shops, and so on, but even rights of way can be altered. The publisher would welcome notes of any such changes.

Mountain walking can be a dangerous activity, carrying a risk of personal injury or death. It should be undertaken only by those with a full understanding of the risks and with the training and/or experience to evaluate them. Whilst every care and effort has been taken in the preparation of this book, the user should be aware that conditions can be highly variable and can change quickly, thus materially affecting the seriousness of a mountain walk.

Therefore, except for any liability which cannot be excluded by law, neither Cicerone nor the author accept liability for damage of any nature (including damage to property, personal injury or death) arising directly or indirectly from the information in this book.

Front cover: The Matterhorn seen from the route above Trift

CONTENTS

The Trek

Map Key

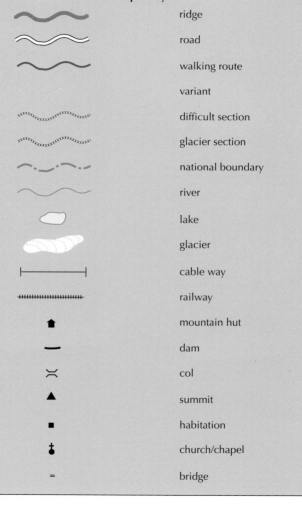

	ridge
	road
	walking route
	variant
	difficult section
	glacier section
	national boundary
	river
	lake
	glacier
	cable way
	railway
	mountain hut
	dam
	col
	summit
	habitation
	church/chapel
	bridge

Old wooden barns, grassy meadows and that mountain – classic Zermatt (Stage 7)

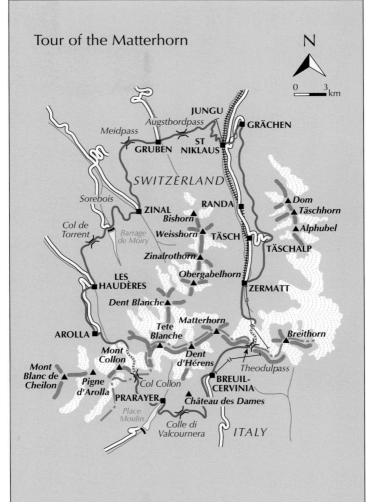

Tour of the Matterhorn

N

0 3 km

JUNGU

GRÄCHEN

Augstbordpass

Meidpass

GRUBEN

ST NIKLAUS

SWITZERLAND

Sorebois

ZINAL

RANDA

Bishorn ▲

▲ *Dom*
▲ *Täschhorn*

Col de Torrent

Barrage de Moiry

Weisshorn ▲

TÄSCH

▲ *Alphubel*

TÄSCHALP

Zinalrothorn ▲

LES HAUDÈRES

Obergabelhorn ▲

ZERMATT

Dent Blanche ▲

AROLLA

Tete Blanche

Matterhorn ▲

▲ *Breithorn*

Mont Collon ▲

Dent d'Hérens ▲

Theodulpass

Mont Blanc de Cheilon ▲

Pigne d'Arolla ▲

Col Collon

BREUIL-CERVINIA

PRARAYER

Château des Dames ▲

Place Moulin

Colle di Valcournera

ITALY

Lots of places enjoy great views of the Matterhorn;
this is at the Grindjisee

INTRODUCTION

Described by Ruskin as the 'most noble cliff in Europe', at 4478m the Matterhorn is neither the highest Alpine summit, nor the most difficult, but worldwide this peak represents the classic mountain. Even if people don't know its name, they've seen its shape replicated on anything from chocolate boxes to corporate adverts. Ask a child to draw a mountain and that's what they'll draw – a pointed pyramid reaching to the sky. The Matterhorn – or Monte Cervino as the Italians call it – represents what is inaccessible, beautiful, the spirit of the summit, the ultimate goal.

Many people aspire to climb it, and some succeed. However, the best views of the Matterhorn and its surrounding summits are to be had not from the flanks of the mountain but from the hillsides that face it. The Tour of the Matterhorn will take you to the most stunning viewpoints from which to marvel at this most unique summit.

To circumnavigate the peak involves quite a long route through the Swiss and Italian Alps. Three cultures will be visited: German-speaking Wallis Switzerland, French-speaking Valais Switzerland, and the Italian Valle d'Aosta. This is not simply a trek to view the Matterhorn; there are many more treats in store. Six valleys are crossed and more than 25 peaks surpassing 4000m will be seen, summits whose soaring buttresses and steep, brooding faces have inspired climbers and trekkers from all over the world.

It is worth taking the time to enjoy the unique aspects of the region, exploring the villages, the local specialities, the differences in architecture and farming. Each area has its own peculiarities, and these deserve to be discovered. The Tour of the Matterhorn enables the walker to immerse himself in the region in a way that is impossible for anyone who just passes through by car. This is a region of stark visual contrasts: high peaks, ice and snow buttresses glinting in the sun, their glaciers formed by unfathomable depths of ice; lush green meadows where cattle graze as they did centuries ago; deep wooded valleys dotted with small villages and towns, ranging from the most old-fashioned to the most modern Alpine resorts.

THE TOUR OF THE MATTERHORN

The Tour of the Matterhorn was originally the idea of the Swiss organisation Valrando (Association Valaisanne de la Randonnée Pédestre). Following the 50th anniversary of the Tour du Mont Blanc (set up in 1952), the president of Valrando, Willy Felay, envisaged the Matterhorn Tour. This tour was seen as providing a liaison between the two neighbouring

The first view of the Matterhorn in Italy, on the trail leading to Breuil-Cervinia (Stage 6)

mountain regions of Valais and the Valle d'Aosta. The route was worked out with the help of Palmira Orsières, director of La Traccia, an organisation that – amongst other things – is responsible for walking in the Aosta Valley region.

The *communes* encountered on the tour have committed to the waymarking and upkeep of the paths and to welcoming walkers who pass through. This tour is envisaged as bringing life to the villages on both sides of the mountains.

The Tour of the Matterhorn is regarded as a relatively 'new' tour, as it has been documented only in the last few years. However, the trek takes in many ancient trails which have linked the Swiss and Italian valleys together for centuries. On this trek the walker becomes a traveller again, crossing cols and frontiers that were used in the old days by porters, soldiers, peasants, traders, pilgrims and bandits. The trek is quite rigorous and weather conditions have a strong influence. The crossing of some passes requires glacier-travel techniques, and the high altitude traversed requires a good level of fitness.

This tour is considerably more demanding than the Tour du Mont Blanc but forms a good progression for those who have already done some Alpine hiking of this type. At 145km the Tour of the Matterhorn is long and should not be rushed. Those with limited time would do better to reduce their trek rather than try to complete the whole thing in a hurry. Ideas for shorter versions are given in the Short Walks section.

Here the tour is divided into seven stages. These are not daily stages, but logical stages, normally from one valley to another. There are usually several accommodation possibilities and hence various ways in which the stages can be divided up. If you choose to do the whole route you can expect to take about 10 days; if you have time you can always take longer. It is difficult to avoid a couple of half days, but in a trek this long that's probably no bad thing. If you choose to use all lift possibilities, do long days and to take the shortest options, the trek can be completed in seven days – but it seems a shame to rush it.

The Tour of the Matterhorn coincides with two other long-distance treks. From Zermatt to Arolla it follows the Walker's Haute Route Trail, and from Breuil-Cervinia to Grächen it takes the Tour of Monte Rosa. Those wishing to do these treks at some future date may wish to miss out these sections, but there are variations for some parts so doing the stages twice may give a chance to cover all options.

Whilst the treks in this region are becoming more popular they have not achieved the fame of the Tour du Mont Blanc, and are unlikely to do so, being rather more arduous and involving more complicated terrain. On many parts of the tour you will experience relative solitude and can expect to see plenty of wildlife.

So, where to start? Since it's a circular tour, theoretically it can be started anywhere along its length, but clearly some places are easier to get to. It is usually nice to start and finish somewhere accessible transport-wise, where you can leave excess gear, buy picnic food and celebrate at the end. To my mind it's good to do this tour with views of the Matterhorn at the start and finish, so the route is described from Zermatt. The French information recommends starting from St Niklaus or Gruben-Meiden, but do you really want to start and finish a trek when the main feature is out of sight?

Next decision – which direction to go in? It's generally done anticlock-wise, and since I can't think of any reason not to go this way that's what I've described. It seems to work that way, and also means that the highest altitude comes at the end when you're fully acclimatised.

THE REGION

The Matterhorn is situated near to the Mischabel and Monte Rosa massifs in the Pennine Alps, bordering southern Switzerland and northern Italy. Extending eastwards from the Col Ferret to the Simplon Pass this huge

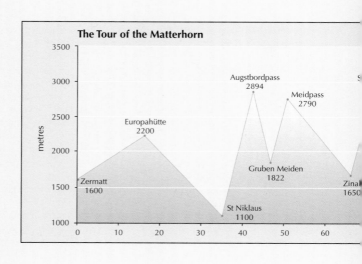

range contains the largest concentration of peaks over 4000m in Europe. The Swiss–Italian frontier forms the Alpine watershed and the most grandiose summits are to be found here, their huge glaciers snaking down into the valleys, on the Swiss side flowing down to the Rhône, on the Italian side draining to the Po.

The enormous barrier of the Pennine Alps represents the pressure zone created when the African tectonic plate collided with the Continental plate. Mountains were forced up and consequent erosion has produced the incredibly spectacular scenery that exists today. Peaks such as Liskamm, the 10 summits of Monte Rosa, the Täschhorn, Dom and Weisshorn (to mention just a few), whilst slightly less lofty than their famous neighbour Mont Blanc, are at least equal in grandeur and splendour.

The Tour of the Matterhorn owes much of its variety and interest to the fact that it visits two distinct regions: the Swiss region of Valais/Wallis and the Italian Valle d'Aosta. Although these two regions are physically close and have a shared history of trade, agriculture and simple survival in this harsh mountain environment, there are many contrasts of culture, architecture, food, language and traditions. Passing from one country to the other you will be struck immediately by the

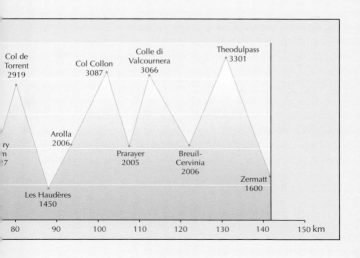

Taking a break before descending to Zinal (Stage 3)

differences in landscape, architecture and farming methods before you even hear any language spoken.

Walking through the mountains and the valleys, and passing through the villages, will give you a chance to discover what makes each valley unique, as well as experiencing the common cultures that unite the region.

ANCIENT PASSES

Many of the trails used by the Tour of the Matterhorn have been used for centuries for many different purposes. Before motorised transport it was often easier to go over the high mountain passes than to descend to the main valleys such as the Rhône and Aosta. Frequently the mountain valleys were rendered impassable by deep gorges, or were prone to rockfall

or landslides. Whilst the high passes carried their own risks – such as bad weather, cold, exhaustion, and attack from marauders – they were usually more direct and less tortuous.

There were abundant reasons for wanting to travel from one valley to the next:

- Trade: in times past people bartered goods rather than dealing in money. Goods that were needed in the Alps included salt and spices, so the mountain people would take their own goods to trade. The wines from the Aosta Valley were sent over to the Valais and Tarentaise by the so-called Route des Vins (which went from Chambave to the Rhône Valley, probably across the Theodul and Collon passes).

Male ibex jostle for dominance on rocks near Trift

- The farmers would take their cattle over into neighbouring valleys to graze as part of the transhumance method of farming.
- People travelled surprisingly long distances for work; for example, much of the Alpine architecture in Switzerland is based on the work of Italian builders from the Valsesia region, near Alagna.
- Sometimes people needed to migrate because they had too many enemies in their native valley, or conditions had made survival there untenable.

One very interesting fact that has emerged from the passage of populations over high passes is that in the Middle Ages the Alpine climate was certainly warmer by degrees than it is today. The Theodulpass, for example, would seem to have been a major route in Roman times, and given the artefacts found there must have been less glaciated than it is today. There have certainly been periods of warmer climate in the past.

Despite these warmer phases, other periods saw mini ice ages; and the vagaries of Alpine weather meant that any excursion into the hills brought with it a risk of bad weather, not to mention illness or even attack. These people really had to want to make the journey, and often not from choice; their lives depended on it.

History tantalises us with fascinating stories about these travels – fortunes lost, treasures found, lives risked. Now as we trek through these

mountains, generally comfortable in our high-tech gear and with well-filled stomachs, it's interesting to try to imagine the trepidation that travellers hundreds of years ago would have felt before setting out on these highly risky ventures. The frequent presence of chapels and crosses en route attests to the need to put their lives in God's hands. Hence on several cols in the Alps – such as the Grand St Bernard, Petit St Bernard and Simplon – we find hospices, erected by religious people to provide safe haven for those poor souls in need of food, shelter or security whilst trying to get to the next valley.

GLACIERS

Glaciers and glaciated mountains are a major feature of the Tour of the Matterhorn, both in terms of the views enjoyed and the terrain encountered.

Heading up the Haut Glacier d'Arolla en route to the Col Collon (Stage 5)

This pass is one of the most famous in the western Alps. In Roman times it was called 'Silvius', and it is documented as early as AD3.

In 1895, 54 coins dating from 2BC to AD4 were found just below the col, and these are now in an archaeological museum in Zermatt. It must certainly have been hotter and drier in those days, since artefacts attest to the passage of the col on foot and on horseback. There was a small settlement on the col providing provisions and guided passage. From the 5th century onwards winters became more rigorous and the glaciers began to expand. Commercial caravans abandoned the route, but from the 9th century the glaciers regressed and there was a return of activity, with several monastic orders settling on both sides of the massif. The Little Ice Age from the 16th century onwards led to colder conditions and the glaciers grew accordingly. Cols such as the Theodulpass became more and more difficult to cross.

The chapel en route to the Theodulpass, now dedicated to Italian Alpinist Franco Bontadini

The col's title dates from this time; it was named after Saint Theodul, who was present in the region around 1688. Would-be travellers regularly fell victim to severe weather whilst attempting this passage, be it from the cold, avalanches, or crevasses. In 1825 a merchant fell in a crevasse with his horse, allegedly taking 10,000 francs with him – an incentive for bounty hunters for years to come.

Horace Benedict de Saussure (famed as the main instigator of the first ascent of Mont Blanc) came this way, and at the col apparently found the remains of an old fort built in 1688 by the Comte de Savoie.

The 20th century saw conditions become easier on the col – in 1910 a herd of 34 cows successfully made the passage – but, nevertheless, care must be taken here.

The valleys have been carved out by the ice, and many people now come to the Alps to marvel at what remains of these huge frozen rivers.

Glaciers respond to climatic change. In cold periods with heavy snowfall, glaciers expand downwards, only to retreat in warm dry periods. In the course of the centuries the climate has changed more than once, influencing the life of the Alpine populations.

The Middle Ages were a time of relative warmth which favoured the colonisation of the Alps at increasingly high altitudes. Glaciers retreated considerably and artefacts found at now glaciated passes attest to the fact that much of this terrain was ice-free for many centuries. The 17th century saw the beginning of the Little Ice Age, a cold period of heavy snowfall which lasted three centuries and saw an impressive regain of territory by the glaciers. Little is known about the consequences, but they were certainly negative for the inhabitants of the Alps. The most significant phenomenon was the advance of the glaciers which buried many of the high pastures and caused panic among the local people. The ice was literally pushing up against their front doors, and they were moved to call the priests to exorcise these demonic forces.

The mid 19th century saw the start of the warm period that has continued, with occasional colder intervals, to this day. Whether we are

now in a natural cycle, or whether the recent fast melting of the glaciers is due to the effects of modern civilisation, is still a moot point.

HOW TO USE THIS GUIDE

This guide has resulted from several trips around the tour, plus years of walking in the region. However, no doubt some things along the route will have changed already; if you come across anything please let me know by sending an email or letter to Cicerone. Use this book as a tool to plan your trip. Once on the tour a map, compass and willingness to adapt to conditions are all essential; the book is not enough on its own.

For this guide the Tour of the Matterhorn has been divided into seven stages. These are not necessarily one-day **stages**, and may need two days or more. I have chosen to describe the route this way so as to give each individual the choice of how to plan the trek.

Each stage has an **introduction**, followed by the details for that stage:

- **starting and finishing points**
- **altitudes, highpoint, distance** in kilometres
- **time**
- **maps** needed
- **transport** options
- **accommodation**
- **extra information** that may be pertinent.

Variants are also noted, and each stage also has **escape routes**

Walking down to Arolla (Stage 4 link route)

briefly described along with transport options to regain the start point. The accommodation is noted by name, but details (phone numbers, fax numbers and Internet sites) are given in Appendix II.

Time for each stage is calculated roughly on the basis of climbing 300m every hour; the ascent time is halved for descent; where there are long flat sections these are calculated on a rate of 4km per hour. These times are given as a rough guide but should not be taken as anything other than that – this is not a challenge! Times are often noted on signposts in Switzerland, and may vary from those given in this guide. Equally you may find your own

times do not match those given – after a day or so you'll have figured out your own rate of progress, so if there is a wild difference between your times and the times in this book, adjust your planning accordingly.

The distance of a stage is difficult to calculate as there are often many zigzags on the ground that are not shown on the map. The kilometre distance noted is the nearest I can get, but will not be exact.

Sketch maps accompany each stage. These are designed as a planning aid, and to show where the route goes. Relevant details have been noted on the maps but these are *not* a substitute for the real thing. When walking

21

this route you need to take the relevant maps, and a compass, and know how to use them.

Route profiles are provided to give a rough idea of the ups and downs encountered along the way.

The section **Short Walks** suggests short variations of the trek, as well as some good walks from the main bases of Zermatt and Breuil-Cervinia. You will find local guidebooks to local walks, and the tourist offices are always good sources for information on pleasant rest-day strolls or interesting explorations.

This book contains a fair amount of **information** that is not strictly relevant to the trek, but which provides background detail about the history and nature of the region. You may only choose to read these sections when stuck in a hut on a wet afternoon with no reading material other than dog-eared out-of-date Alpine

Club magazines printed in a language you don't understand!

Safety and rescue and **glacier travel** are all covered in the guide; see Appendix V for information on the latter. The glaciers encountered on this trek are, however, relatively innocuous. You do need to rope up, and you do need crampons, but this is not major mountaineering.

The **Appendices** contain additional information: further reading, accommodation details, glossary of phrases and terms, tourist office and guides' office information. Do please appreciate that these numbers and Internet details were correct at the time of writing, but that details do change. If a number doesn't work, or an email comes flying back 'undeliverable' from cyber space, get on Google and do a search.

Haymaking at Jungu (Stage 2)

PRACTICALITIES

WHEN TO GO

The Tour of the Matterhorn crosses cols of over 3000m, where snow is likely to remain until well into June. The huts used on the trek generally do not open until late June or early July, so it is not advisable to set out before the summer Alpine season begins. However, later is not necessarily better as certain areas benefit from a coating of snow to disguise the horrors of denuded ski resorts, which are far more acceptable in their winter garb.

You have to decide if you plan to walk every part of the route, or whether you intend to take the occasional lift, for example from Breuil-Cervinia to Testa Grigia. This section of the trek is quite ugly when there is no snow, but such conditions do allow you to walk up to the slopes. When névé remains walking may be more difficult – either because the snow is hard and slippery, or because it's a hot, late afternoon, the snow has partially melted, and therefore doesn't hold your weight.

If you're planning to take lifts be sure to check their open season.

The best time to do this trek is therefore during this brief summer holiday season. The earlier you go the more flowers will be in bloom on the hillsides; the middle of the season sees the most holidaymakers in the Alps; the end is generally noted for beautiful autumn light, but can be prone to fresh snowfall above 3000m.

If in doubt call local tourist offices or the huts for up-to-date information on conditions.

HOW TO GET THERE

Zermatt
By air
The nearest airports to the Tour of the Matterhorn are Zurich and Geneva.
From Britain **Zurich** is served by:

British Airways www.ba.com tel: 0844 4930787

Easyjet www.easyjet.com tel: 0870 600 0000

Swiss International www.swiss.com tel: 0845 601 0956

Swiss International also operates from the USA and most other airports worldwide.

Zurich airport is found on www.zurich-airport.com

Many airlines fly into Geneva from Britain:

British Airways www.ba.com tel: 0844 4930787

Easyjet www.easyjet.com tel: 0870 600 0000

jet2 www.jet2.com tel: 0870 737 8282

Swiss International www.swiss.com tel: 0845 601 0956

BmiBaby www.bmibaby.com tel: 0870 264 0224

From America: Swiss International (sharing with American Airlines), Continental and Lufthansa (sharing with United Airlines).

From Ireland: Aer Lingus www.aerlingus.com tel: +353 1 886 8844.

Geneva airport can be found on www.gva.ch tel: +41 22 717 71 11 info@gva.ch

Onward travel to Zermatt is best by **train**. The Swiss railway network is incredibly efficient; timetables and online ticket sales can be found at www.sbb.ch

By train
If you choose to travel out to Switzerland by train then you will not be disappointed by the service once there. It may be worth buying a Swiss rail pass; the Swiss Tourist Office in your home country will be able to advise (UK tel: 0207 734 1921). All the different passes are described in detail on www.myswissalps.com/swissrailpasses

The preferred mode of transport in Zermatt

A lovely grassy trail leads down to
Rifugio Prarayer at the end of Stage 5

By car
If you drive to Switzerland you'll need to buy a motorway 'vignette' on entry to the country, which currently costs 40chf for the year. You cannot take the car to Zermatt, but must park at Täsch and take the train up to the town.

Bus
Eurolines offer a regular service from Britain and Ireland to Switzerland, serving both Geneva and Zurich. Whilst the journey is long the price is competitive: www.eurolines.com tel: 020 7730 8235.

Breuil-Cervinia
By air
The nearest airport is **Turin**, tel: +39.011.5676361/2 **www.aeroportoditorino.it**

Turin airport is served by:
Ryanair www.ryanair.com tel: 0871 246 0000

Easyjet www.easyjet.com tel: 0870 600 0000

British Airways www.ba.com tel: 0844 4930787

Coming to Italy from outside Europe the nearest airport is Milan.

By train
Turin is served by train and is on the railway route to Aosta. From there good bus services run up the valley

to Breuil-Cervinia. There is no direct connection from Turin or Milan to Cervinia. To reach Cervinia you have to change bus at Chatillon. The bus stations are in the city and not at the airports.

By car
Driving in Italy is generally good fun so long as you have an adventurous spirit. The motorways usually charge tolls.

Bus
Eurolines offer a regular service from Britain and Ireland to Italy with stops at Turin and Aosta and Chatillon, which is at the bottom of the valley up to Cervinia. Whilst the journey is long the price is competitive: www.eurolines.com tel: 020 7730 8235.

From Zurich, Geneva or Turin airports you can reach any of the other towns encountered during the trek. In Switzerland the train is the best option for getting along the main valleys, then the yellow PTT buses give access to all but the remotest villages. These tend to meet up with the trains, so travel is exceptionally easy. Italy is a different story; here the bus seems to be the best option.

ACCOMMODATION

There are a host of possibilities for your stay in the region, ranging from hotels of all standards to *gîtes* to huts to campsites. In the summer season – July and August – there is a huge demand for accommodation, so advance booking is highly recommended (see Appendix II). **Note that on a trek such as this it is important to get your provisions for the day before you set out in the morning; on some stages there is no guarantee that you will be able to buy food during the day.**

Hotels

These range from 4-star luxury to no-star basic. Major towns such as Zermatt and Breuil-Cervinia have many to choose from, whereas the small villages will just have a handful, usually in the 2-star or below category. In addition to rooms, some hotels also have a dormitory; this is particularly common in Switzerland. There may even be a kitchen where you can cook your own meals, but this is less usual. The local tourist offices will provide a list of hotels and may even make bookings for you.

Campsites

There are sites in most Alpine towns. Camping is generally not allowed in the valley outside of campsites. Ask the tourist office for details.

Huts or refuges

Mountain huts vary greatly in the facilities they offer, from quite luxurious with showers and even rooms to the most basic with just a dormitory and a dining room. There are always toilets, and running cold water is almost guaranteed (although the exceptionally hot summer of 2003 did see a few isolated cases of dried-up water supplies). Huts high in the mountains may not have running

The rather grand Hotel Schwarzhorn (Stage 2)

water early in the morning when the source could be frozen, so it's wise to fill water bottles the previous evening. Most huts are open from late June to early September, and there will be a guardian in residence, who usually cooks an evening meal and provides breakfast. At a few huts you can take your own food, but you must make sure the guardian is happy with this. Quite frankly it is hardly worth the effort of carrying up food when a very good meal will be on offer for a reasonable price. Drinks – alcoholic and otherwise – are also sold.

In Italy there are strict laws about public water supplies and in some huts you may be told the tap water is not controlled – this means they cannot guarantee that it is clean.

Hut etiquette

We are privileged in the Alps to have a system of huts that enables us to walk just carrying small packs, knowing that at the end of each day we'll have somewhere to sleep and a good hot meal. It's really important that we treat the huts and their guardians with the respect that they deserve. I highly recommend that you book accommodation in advance, even if you just phone the night before; and if you are not going to show up do call to cancel. When you arrive at a hut make yourself known to the guardian and let him show you what to do. Each hut has its own system; some are very relaxed, others less so. The guardian will tell you where to leave your sac:

sometimes you can take it to your room, sometimes not. He will ask you to take off your boots and show you where to put them, as well as where to leave crampons and trekking poles. You are expected to vacate your room by a certain time in the morning and to leave it as you found it; this generally means folding up blankets or quilts.

If you have particular dietary requirements tell the guardian when you arrive so he can prepare a suitable meal. Most huts do not have a huge variety of food available, so unless you really are a vegetarian it's best to eat whatever you are given. Huts do sell drinks, and sometimes you can run up a tab and pay for everything at the end of your stay. Many huts prefer that you settle the bill before going to bed. Remember that credit cards are not usually accepted, so take cash.

Although sometimes the guardian and friends may party til the small hours it's generally accepted that from 10pm everyone is in bed.

Most huts do not have road access, so everything has to be transported up by helicopter or on foot. Bear this in mind and take your own rubbish down.

LANGUAGES

The Matterhorn and associated peaks lie on the Swiss–Italian border. Whilst you will find that in the main centres of Breuil-Cervinia – and especially Zermatt – English is widely understood it is nevertheless

Viewed from the Höhbalmen trail above Zermatt the Matterhorn looks especially fine

Pleasant walking on dry glacier (Stage 5)

worth making an effort to speak the local languages. Shopkeepers and hoteliers have realised that it serves them well to speak English, and most do to some extent. Not withstanding this, it is worth making the effort to learn a few basic words; there is a lot of pleasure to be gained by having a go at communicating in the local language. Generally people will meet you halfway and will respect your endeavours in the realm of international relations!

In the Swiss part of the walk you will hike in both German- and French-speaking Switzerland, and the languages do not really overlap. From Zermatt to the Meidpass or Forcletta (Stage 3) German (or more precisely Swiss-German) is spoken, then it changes to French. From the Col Collon onwards Italian is used, all the way back to the Theodulpass.

Some useful words are noted in the Glossary and Useful Terms (Appendix IV), and those relating to the weather can be especially useful if you do not manage to find a forecast in English.

CURRENCIES

With the introduction of the Euro it has become very easy to travel around Europe, although some consider it to be a bit dull – gone are the heady days when you had to go armed with millions of Italian lire to buy a loaf of bread! In Switzerland, however, the Swiss franc remains the currency, but some cafés and supermarkets will accept Euros if that's all you have with you. The same applies to Swiss mountain huts, but don't expect to get a good rate of exchange. Change will generally be given in francs.

In the big towns credit cards are generally accepted and travellers' cheques can be cashed. There are also ATMs. However, bear in mind that there are really only two centres that fit these criteria on the trek: Breuil-Cervinia and Zermatt. In addition there are banks, as well as all other facilities, at Evolène, 3km off the route at Les Haudères, and at Grimentz in the Val d'Anniviers (Stage 4). Valpelline is probably too far from Prarayer to serve a similar purpose – you'd have to make a long detour to get there – unless bad weather has closed in.

DIFFICULTY OF THE TRAIL

The Tour of the Matterhorn takes in non-glaciated and glaciated terrain. As glaciers go, the ones crossed on this trek are relatively gentle slopes, and the gear and experience needed is covered elsewhere in the book (see also Appendix V). The rest of the trek is generally waymarked. The trails are quite rough and rocky in places, and occasionally the steeper sections have been equipped with metal rungs and/or cables. These sections are short and not difficult, although in rain or snow they would be a bit slippery.

MAPS

There is now a dedicated Tour of the Matterhorn map: Tour of the Matterhorn **1:50,000** Edition IG IVRN available at Wega bookshop in Zermatt. Other **1:50,000** maps: Carte Nationale de la Suisse 5006 Matterhorn Mischabel; Istituto Geografico Centrale 5 Cervino-Matterhorn e Monte Rosa.

1:25,000 maps: Carte Nationale de la Suisse 1328 Randa; 1308 St Niklaus; 1307 Vissoie; 1327 Evolène; 1347 Matterhorn; 1348 Zermatt; Istituto Geografico Centrale 108 Cervino Matterhorn Breuil-Cervinia, Champoluc.

1:30,000 map: Istituto Geografico Centrale 115 La Valpelline, Valle di Ollomont, Valle di St Barthelemy. **Note** Although this map is 1:30,000 I have used it as a 1:25,000 map as there is no alternative.

Maps are available locally, or from:
The Map Shop
Freephone: 0800 085 40 80;
tel: 01684 593146
Fax: 01684 594559
e-mail: themapshop@btinternet.com
www.themapshop.co.uk

Stanfords
Tel: 0207 836 1321
Fax: O207 836 0189
e-mail:
customer.services@stanfords.co.uk
www.stanfords.co.uk

FOOTPATHS AND WAYMARKS

The Tour of the Matterhorn has been very well signed and publicised since its inauguration in 2002. To my horror, for a few months during its setting up large signs appeared along some paths,

You're unlikely to miss this turn-off en route to Perrucca-Vuillermoz (Stage 6)

Swiss signposts are always very precise

announcing that you were indeed on the Tour of the Matterhorn. Thankfully these have now disappeared and the trail has settled down. In Switzerland the paths are generally waymarked in red and white paint flashes, indicating that this is a long-distance trek. In Italy the waymarks are yellow.

However, do not expect simply to step onto the path and follow the paint flashes until the end of the tour. This would be reckless and, surely, part of the fun of hiking is to use the map and decide which route to take. There are quite often route options, or you may decide you'd like to include a nearby summit or visit an interesting village. Equally some path junctions are not signed – thank goodness. Having said that, if you plan to follow the main trail and the path you're on is very indistinct you should check to see if you haven't missed a turning. Although most of the trails for the Tour of the Matterhorn are well used, you do need to use a map. Fog and snow can occur at any time in the

Alps, and at such times those friendly little paint flashes tend to disappear. It is important to try to stay on the path as the terrain 'off piste' can be very rough and difficult. In snow or bad visibility you will need to use map and compass (and maybe GPS if that's what you're used to).

The Italian maps often number footpaths, and whilst these may correspond to numbers painted on the trail signs, do not bank on it. It's far better to use the map to see which direction a path should take rather than trying to blindly follow unreliable numbers on the ground.

LIFTS AND BUSES

There are several possibilities for using a variety of lifts during the Tour of the Matterhorn. These can be very useful for several reasons:

- If you are pressed for time using a lift could cut off several hours of walking and enable you to cover more ground that day.

- If knees are hurting, taking a lift down could make all the difference to the rest of the trip.
- Lifts are inevitably in ski areas, some of which look a lot better in winter when covered in snow. It's a bit like removing clothes from a body that is best left dressed – inadvisable to say the least! So to avoid walking up bulldozed pistes it may be a good idea to take the lift – the ascent from Plan Maison to the Theodulpass springs to mind.

However, it is important to bear in mind that the lifts have a very limited open season in the summer. Typically this may be from the first week of July to the first week of September, so if these are an integral part of your trek planning you need to be absolutely sure they will be running. If they are just an option this is less crucial. Nevertheless, do bear in mind that once you've decided to take a lift, finding it closed can be a very traumatic experience! It's worth knowing that some lifts have a timetable in the summer (rather than running continuously), and they tend to close for lunch.

Buses are a useful means of escape if you have to abandon the trek for some reason, or if you only plan to do part of it. Most of the bus services mentioned here are year-round regular services, but the frequency can change radically outside the high summer season. Tourist offices will have details.

This flat rock below Forcletta provides a pleasant resting place (Stage 3 variant)

SAFETY

EMERGENCIES AND RESCUE

Rescue telephone numbers: Europe 112; Switzerland 144; Italy 118

Whilst trekking should not be a high-risk activity there are increasing numbers of accidents, even on non-glaciated terrain. This is partly because more and more people walk in the Alps, but it is also a factor of the adventurous terrain that is being accessed by footpaths. Glaciated terrain brings its own objective hazards, but these are minimal on the gentle slopes encountered on the Tour of the Matterhorn. Nevertheless, for all Alpine walking you need to consider emergencies that could arise. If you are well equipped and prepared you will hopefully avoid, or at least know how to deal with, most situations.

Note There are no pharmacy facilities between Zermatt and Cervinia (at least seven days' walking).

First aid

All walkers should carry a basic first aid kit in their rucksacks. However, although the trek described here is multi-day, there are opportunities to get medical supplies if needed or to abandon the route for a few days. In addition there are good and reliable rescue services in the Swiss and Italian regions covered, so the first aid kit can be kept to the essentials:

- plasters
- painkillers
- aspirin
- treatment for diarrhoea
- antiseptic cream
- crêpe bandage
- fly repellent
- antihistamine cream
- scissors
- tweezers
- antiseptic wipes
- wound dressing
- blister kit
- latex gloves
- triangular bandage (or use a scarf or bandana)
- bivvy bag or space blanket (shiny foil)

This kit allows treatment of most emergencies that could be encountered during this walk. Resourcefulness is most useful: for example, a trekking pole can be used to splint an injured arm or leg. However, if a problem becomes serious then you should be prepared to leave the trek. It is not recommended to continue if, for example, you have an upset stomach which prevents you eating properly or risks leading to dehydration, or some form of infection, such as a blister that has become ulcerated. Continuing to hike day after day with an ongoing condition could cause long-term damage.

Potential problems on the hill

As well as carrying the gear it's also crucial to know what to do in the event of incidents that can happen during mountain walks:

Heart attack Everyone should have basic first aid knowledge. Treatment of a heart attack victim goes beyond the scope of this guide but should be learnt at a first aid centre. This is knowledge that hopefully is never used, hence the need for regular refresher courses.

Hypothermia If you are walking in the summer months you would not expect to be at risk of hypothermia, which is generally associated with winter expeditions and high-altitude mountaineering. However, there are a surprising number of incidences of hypothermia each summer in the non-glaciated Alps. In addition, on the Tour of the Matterhorn you are flirting with the high mountains and attaining altitudes of nearly 3500m. In classic summer hypothermia cases the victim becomes very hot and consequently sweaty whilst walking uphill, then cools very quickly, exacerbated by wind chill and tiredness. The same situation can arise during bad weather, when snow is frequent above 2000m even in the summer. The victim's core body temperature drops slightly, and the body's response is to cut off circulation to the outer extremities. Hands and feet become very cold; the victim starts to shiver and to become irrational, unable to make basic decisions

such as stopping to eat and put on warm clothes. Eventually a comatose state is reached, and death will follow quickly.

The best action to take against hypothermia is to avoid it in the first place. When the summit is reached or the wind gets up, put on an extra layer straight away; don't hesitate to change your planned route if necessary. The symptoms of impending hypothermia (sometimes referred to as exposure in the early stages) should be recognised and dealt with as soon as possible: give the victim warm drinks and food and put on clothing; a hat will prevent considerable heat loss. If feasible the walk should be cut short to get the victim down to the valley for warmth and rest. If the situation has already become more serious, with the victim displaying irrational and aggressive behaviour, it is imperative to act quickly. Once the stage of coma is reached the rescue service must be called as the group cannot move the victim themselves. At this stage the victim must be kept warm, insulated from the ground as well as from the elements, and not moved.

Altitude sickness It is unlikely that true altitude sickness will be encountered on the Tour of the Matterhorn as mostly the trail remains around and below 3000m. Whilst people may sometimes think they are feeling the effects of the high altitude, altitude sickness is really only encountered above 3000m.

35

Summit of the Breithorn (Stage 7 variant)

However, those coming from sea level will certainly feel breathless the first day or so hiking in the Alps. To what extent this is due to the thinner air and to what extent to the inclines is a moot issue. Were you to start immediately with an ascent of the Breithorn it is very likely that you would feel bad, and serious sickness is a possibility. When going high be sure to drink plenty of water and, if necessary, take small doses of aspirin for headaches. Remember to keep to lower altitudes for the first days of a holiday.

Falls The outcome of a fall can range from minor scrapes and grazes to sprained and broken limbs, or worse. The former are easily treated with dressings and antiseptic creams. Sprains can be strapped up effectively, and the victim can usually make his way down with help. Broken limbs can be splinted using a trekking pole, but whether the victim can walk down depends on where the break is and the severity of it: if in doubt call the rescue service. Anything worse requires help from professionals; back and head injuries are potentially very serious so the victim should not be moved (unless by staying where they are further injury is likely) and the rescue service should be called immediately.

Rescue
Should the unthinkable happen and you do have to call the rescue services, it's reassuring to know that compared to many mountain areas the Alps are relatively friendly in an accident situation. Given good weather you can expect the mountain rescue to arrive within a short time of your call. In Switzerland and Italy

there are professional rescue services, using trained rescue personnel, doctors and Guides. They generally operate with helicopters from a base very near town. Only in bad weather will the helicopter be unable to fly, in which case a rescue party might be sent on foot; this could take a lot longer.

However, calling the rescue should be seen as a last resort. Since mobile phones have become part of the walker's kit list the rescue get called out for the most trivial of reasons, ranging from tiredness to being late for a restaurant reservation. It should be remembered that having the back-up of such a service is a privilege not to be abused.

In the case of a genuine need for rescue use the following procedure.

- Call the rescue services on 112 or:
  Italy Aosta Valley 118
  Switzerland Valais 144
- Have the following information ready:
  1 Your name and mobile phone number
  2 The nature of the accident
  3 The number of victims
  4 The seriousness of the victim's injuries – is he conscious?
  5 Your position, itinerary, altitude
  6 The time of the accident
  The current weather conditions – wind and visibility
- Prepare for the arrival of the helicopter team by putting the injured person somewhere accessible. This will not always be possible but, if feasible, find a flat place where the helicopter can land. Do

Helicopter flying over the Matterhorn

not move an unconscious patient or one who may have back injuries. In all events secure the victim and also all equipment. Keep everyone else away from this area; the helicopter will generate a lot of wind when it arrives.

- Make your position visible, using brightly coloured items such as bivvy bags or rucksacks.
- When the helicopter appears raise your arms in the air to make a Y sign to indicate that you are the people who called for rescue.

Once the team have arrived they will take over. The rescue services in the Alps speak English, so this is probably not the time to try out those new German/French/Italian phrases unless you are reasonably proficient.

It is recommended that in the Alps walkers carry a mobile phone, but only to be used to call the rescue when it is genuinely necessary. There is telephone network cover in much of the Alps, but not everywhere. The telephone does not work over a large part of the Italian Tour of the Matterhorn.

It is vital to know your own number as the rescue service will ask for it.

Insurance

Rescue is not free in Switzerland and Italy, neither are hospital and medical costs. An accident could prove very costly so you need to be insured for rescue from the hill, medical costs

and repatriation. You can get this in your own country before leaving to trek. Make sure the insurance company knows you will be trekking on terrain that is both glaciated and non-glaciated, and for the former you may use a rope. You will not be climbing. If you cannot get appropriate cover at home you can get insurance for the trek period from certain tourist offices – certainly from Zermatt.

EQUIPMENT

For the Tour of the Matterhorn you need to be equipped for regular summer Alpine trekking, but with additional gear for glacier crossings. This can add a significant amount of weight to your sac. If you feel this is too much to carry over the whole trek then consider taking a Guide for the two glaciated sections; the Guide will bring the rope and glacier-travel gear, and the most you will need is a pair of lightweight crampons (see Guided Treks, p44).

Clothing The weather can range from very hot to very cold with everything in between. Normal temperatures at 2000m are about 10–15°C in the day; 0°C is usually between 3000m and 3500m. However, during bad weather or storms the temperature can plummet, and snow can fall as low as 1500m at any time during the summer. Wind will make the conditions feel even colder, so you need to be prepared for all eventualities. Layers are better than padded or thick garments, and clothes next to the skin should be moisture-wicking and quick-drying – leave the cotton T-shirts at home. Life in the hills should be seen as a different experience to your normal home life so embrace the simplicity of it and accept that you may well be wearing the same clothes for days at a time. In this way you can keep your sac weight acceptable – nothing spoils a good walk more than having unwanted kilos piled on your back.

Waterproofs are essential, and a waterproof cover for your sac is a good idea. Ankle-high **gaiters** are the coolest for summer, and are just for use on the glaciers to keep the snow out of your boots. **Gloves** and **fleece hat** will complete the cold-weather ensemble.

The **rucksack** does not need to be huge, especially if you're planning on using huts. However, it does need to be comfortable, and for trekking it's best to have a sac with a padded hip-belt.

Boots can be lightweight so long as they take crampons. The sole is hugely important – it's amazing how a worn sole affects your grip on all sorts of terrain.

Instep crampons are a lightweight alternative for this type of trek

Assuming the weather will be mainly sunny you need to go prepared. At altitude those UV rays are that much stronger as you're higher up and there is less pollution to protect you. A **sunhat**, **sunglasses** and **suncream** are definitely called for.

Sheet sleeping bags are highly recommended for huts (and are a requirement in Italian huts).

Glacier gear Glacier travel involves being roped up and having the necessary gear to get you or someone else out of a crevasse. Crampons are generally needed to walk on glaciers, but it may not be deemed necessary to have an ice axe each – one in the group may

suffice. If you do not plan to ascend any peaks a pair of instep crampons is usually adequate for the Tour of the Matterhorn. These are considerably smaller than normal crampons and can be attached to all footwear.

First aid kit
Trekking poles
Water bottle
Snacks/picnic for the day
Camera
Compass
Maps

GLACIER TRAVEL

Glaciers introduce a whole new dimension to walking, notably that of the dangers of crevasses and the

Roped up near the top of the Haut Glacier d'Arolla (Stage 5).

need to use crampons and possibly an ice axe. With the right equipment and, far more importantly, the right knowledge, these dangers can be reduced to an acceptable level. This knowledge can be gained in part by reading textbooks, but really there is no substitute for the real thing, either by going with experienced friends or by paying for professional instruction by qualified Guides. It is essential that you are trained in glacier travel before venturing onto glaciers during this trek (see Appendix V).

Glacier-travel guidelines
There are two types of glacier conditions:

Dry glacier – when the glacier has no fresh snow cover and is purely ice; all crevasses can be seen

Wet glacier – when fresh snow lies on the ice and hides some or all of the crevasses.

The dry glacier often requires crampons for safe walking but usually, unless it is steep, no rope is required as the crevasses are visible and thus can be avoided. A wet glacier presents more objective dangers as the crevasses are hidden and snow bridges are usually used to cross them – these can be fragile and can collapse at any moment. When you step onto a wet glacier the rule is 'rope up and cover up' – that is, attach the rope and put on long-sleeved shirts, trousers and gloves as a fall into a crevasse could be a very cold experience. A glacier may be

dry in its lower part but become wet higher up, so always take the rope in case – if in doubt, use it.

Be aware of how the **crevasses** have formed on the glacier, and when roped up ensure that you are not all at risk at the same time. Crevasses most commonly occur on the edge of convexities, on the outside and inside of bends, at the confluence of two glaciers and around jutting features such as rocky buttresses that project into the glacier. Usually you can plan your route from looking carefully at the map and trying to avoid these areas, although this doesn't mean you won't find crevasses on flat parts of glaciers. The **rope** should be kept reasonably taut at all times, and especially when crossing obviously crevassed areas and delicate snow bridges.

Some glaciers are threatened from higher up by **seracs**. If you have to walk under a serac wall, go as quickly as possible – this is not a good place to stop for a picnic.

Glaciers are best travelled in the morning, when the snow is firm underfoot and the snow bridges over the crevasses are at their most solid. An **Alpine dawn** is one of the joys of the high mountains, and huts are not the place to have a lie-in since everyone gets up early. If this means you arrive early afternoon at the next hut then enjoy the views and take a nap.

Glacier-travel gear list
Crampons
Ice axe 55–60cm for a normal-size person.
Harness
Crevasse rescue equipment 2 prussik loops, a long sling, 5 karabiners (1 screwgate, 1 pear-shaped screwgate [HMS] which can be used for an Italian hitch, 3 snaplinks), and an ice screw. This is a minimum requirement; you may choose to take other things according to what you're used to.
Rope Dynamic rope of at least 8mm, minimum 30m long. Clearly if there are lots of people in the group more than one rope should be taken, but bear in mind that weight is also an issue. It was thought until recently that a rope should not be used singly if it isn't designed as a single rope,

but on glaciers the force generated by falls is not the same as that generated on rock climbs (it isn't possible to generate factor 2 falls). It is now agreed that 8mm is adequate, provided it is dynamic. However, the downside of a thin rope is that it is harder to grip for rescue manoeuvres, both by hand and with prussiks.

Hiring a guide
For the glacier crossings and the ascent of the Breithorn you need to either have some experience in glacier travel or to hire a Guide. Both Zermatt and Breuil-Cervinia have Guides' bureaux (see Appendix III). In Arolla you can hire a Guide through the Bournissen Sports shop in the village. It is recommended that you reserve a Guide a few days in advance and you need to specify what you are planning.

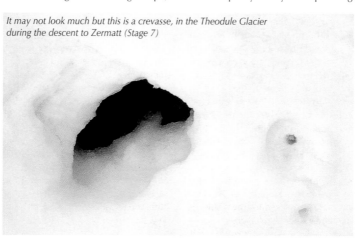

It may not look much but this is a crevasse, in the Theodule Glacier during the descent to Zermatt (Stage 7)

Once the cloud clears after bad weather the fresh snow makes the peaks look even more spectacular

The Guide will generally take up to six people; he will provide the rope and may also bring harnesses and crampons (certainly this is the case for the Breithorn). For this summit you can hire a Guide from either of the huts on the Plateau Rosa. Again, best to do so in advance.

Weather information on the Web

www.meteofrance.com This also provides three-day forecasts for Europe and the world.

Swiss Alps

www.meteoswiss.admin.ch Weather forecast for Switzerland available in French, German and Italian.
www.trs.ch/meteo Romande TV forecast in French for 5 days.
www.sf.tv Swiss-German TV forecast.
www.zermatt.com General information.
www.sac-cas.ch Swiss Alpine Club site; provides lots of useful links.

Italian Alps

www.regione.vda.it Weather forecasts.
www.cai-svi.it Italian Alpine Club site, with mountain weather.

Weather information by phone

Switzerland

Weather: 162 Press 1 when told to then # (diaz) when told to.

Italy (Aosta region)

Weather: 0165 44113

Mountain weather can change very suddenly, and you must always get a weather forecast before heading out. These are available at local tourist offices, Guides' bureaux, by phone or Internet. However, don't stick rigidly to what is predicted; sometimes fronts come in more quickly or more slowly than anticipated (maybe by up to six hours), an anticyclone can hold off a front for longer than expected, or a very localised change can affect the outcome. Look at the sky, and if you can see the weather worsening rethink your plans for that day.

Classic signs include:

• thin wispy clouds caused by high winds at altitude
• increasing wind in the valleys
• cumulus clouds building in the mountains
• locals carrying umbrellas.

Forecasts are generally put out in the local language – a brief glossary of terms is given in Appendix IV – but you can always ask at the local tourist offices, where usually somebody has at least a rudimentary knowledge of English.

Whether the weather has changed over the centuries is a fascinating subject, beyond the scope of this book. However, whilst the weather can certainly be unpredictable there are some relevant general facts.

The mountains are affected by general European weather systems, but they also create their own localised anomalies. As a frontal system approaches the Alps the air, laden with moisture from the sea, has to rise over the mountains, resulting in a cooling of the air, turning water vapour into droplets and consequently precipitation. The precipitation sometimes falls mainly on one side of the Alps, leaving the other in a rain shadow, enjoying relatively dry conditions. This classically happens in the Mont Blanc massif when, for example, the weather can come from the south, giving heavy rain or snow on the Italian side of the range whilst the Chamonix Valley is protected and basks in the sun. The opposite is sometimes true when the weather comes from the north. This effect is caused by a 'fohn' wind: a southern fohn causes rain on the Italian side of the Alps, a northern fohn means that Italy will be largely dry, whilst France and parts of Switzerland get the bad weather.

A front can be accompanied by winds from a different direction, for example a westerly front is often accompanied by a southerly fohn, and frequently the wind changes direction after a front has passed.

So if it's raining in Breuil-Cervinia there's a chance it will be sunny in Zermatt, and vice versa.

GUIDED TREKS

The legal requirement to take people on guided treks on non-glaciated terrain in Europe is the diploma Accompagnateur en Montagne (France) or Accompagnatore di Montagna (Italy). This qualification

Zermatt is dominated by more than the Matterhorn –
here Liskamm, Castor and Pollux provide the backdrop

exists in Switzerland too, but is not yet
legally required. An unqualified person
will not have liability insurance. These
Guides are not only well qualified in
navigation skills and the techniques
for walking and leading groups, they
are also a mine of information about
the region, flora, fauna, geology, history and culture. A day out with such a
Guide should enhance your visit even
if you can find the path perfectly well
yourself.

The British qualification
International Mountain Leader has
equivalence with the European
qualifications, but generally a person resident in the Alps will be the
most informed about the area and the
conditions.

For glaciated terrain a Guide
must hold the UIAGM High Mountain
diploma.

Most guided treks of the Tour
of the Matterhorn will be led by
an Accompagnateur en Montagne
with a UIAGM Guide for the glacier
passages.

45

INFORMATION

Zermatt is a town of contrasts. Dominated by the Matterhorn, it is nowadays assured a place high on the wish list for many people travelling in the Alps. Just seeing the Matterhorn is a must for anyone with any interest in natural beauty.

With the advent of European travel in the 18th century the people of Zermatt quickly became aware that in the Matterhorn they had a potential goldmine, and since that time the town has developed in line with the huge commercial success of the Matterhorn's image. However, if all you do is arrive in Zermatt by train and walk down the main street, jostled by shoppers, to the background sounds of whistling stuffed marmots and the jingle of cowbell keyrings, you will miss much of the charm of the town.

'Zermatt' means 'to the meadows' ('zer', to; 'matt', meadow). However, 500 years ago Zermatt was still called 'Prato Borno', a name given in Roman times, meaning 'cultivated field'. Very little is known about the early history of the region, but Roman artefacts and coins dated between 200BC and AD400 found at the Theodulpass attest to the fact that this was a most important and strategic crossing place at that time. Local documents recount how in 102BC General Marius came over

the Theodulpass and on over the Col d'Hérens to crush the Teutons.

Zermatt has been a settlement since ancient times – apparently as early as AD100 there was a scattering of tiny dwellings there – but until about AD1100 there was no real central settlement. For centuries it was a place of trade and exchange between neighbouring valleys. Zmutt, situated just above Zermatt – today just a small hamlet with a good view and nice restaurants – was in those days the last place en route to the Theodulpass, and thus an important spot with its customs post, inns and guiding service for the passage to the col.

It would seem that the climate began to change as early as the 12th century, and gradually the Theodulpass became impassable for parts of the year. The village that had existed there was abandoned. The 17th and 18th centuries – known as the Little Ice Age – were particularly cold, and the glaciers advanced right down to the valleys. The passage of the cols became impracticable, even in summer. Life was almost impossible in the high villages and many people moved away from their Alpine origins. Evidence of this lies in the fact that in the Middle Ages, to ensure good weather, the villagers of Zermatt had made a vow to send seven Zermatt men over the Col d'Hérens to

Sion every year to pray. This was possible over one long day. By the 17th century this had become a very dangerous undertaking, and in 1660 the local Bishop gave them dispensation and the men just had to go to Täsch to pray instead.

Early in the 1800s climatic conditions began to improve, and for the first time foreigners came to visit the Zermatt Valley. At first they were greeted with hostility and mistrust, but gradually the villagers began to set up inns for these travellers. The first official inn in Zermatt was the Hotel Mont Cervie, which had three beds, and which later became the now renowned Hotel Monte Rosa, run by the famous hotelier Alexandre Seiler. By 1812 there were on average 10 to 12 visitors a year.

Until the carriage road was built from St Niklaus in 1858–1860, Zermatt could only be reached on foot or by mule along a rough path. Yet many illustrious visitors were attracted to the unique experience of the town, amongst them Englehardt (whose books did much to publicise the valley), De Saussure, Ruskin, G.D. Forbes (a renowned cartographer and naturalist), as well as the most talented alpinists of the day, including Edward Whymper. Many came out of curiosity, to study, explore, reflect and climb.

The Matterhorn was a big draw: as one French author put it, 'Le Cervin n'est pas quelque chose, c'est quelqu'un' and he was right. There is only one Matterhorn – and there is nothing else quite like it.

Gateway to the Matterhorn

The arrival of the railway for summer use in 1891 proved to be a real boost to tourism. The introduction of skiing to the Alps in the early 1900s assured the area's future, but also the relentless exploitation of Zermatt, as it did all other Alpine resorts – the 'White Gold', as it was known. An eclectic mix of climbers, writers (including Mark Twain who wrote the amusing *Ascent of the Riffleberg*) and general travellers would flock to Zermatt in ever-increasing numbers until the world wars put paid to most travel.

It was only in the 1960s that the route as far as Täsch was made into a proper road. Zermatt town council agreed that cars would not be allowed into town, and in 1972 the people of Zermatt rejected a proposal for a public road. In 1979 the Klein Matterhorn cable car, at 3820m the highest in Europe, was completed.

THE MATTERHORN

Name

Horace Benedict de Saussure (the main instigator of the first ascent of Mont Blanc) was also the first to attempt to measure the Matterhorn, in 1789. His estimate of 4502m was remarkably close as the peak has two highpoints: the higher Swiss one (4477.5m) and the Italian one, where there is now a cross (4476.4m).

The name 'Matterhorn' comes from the name of the valley leading

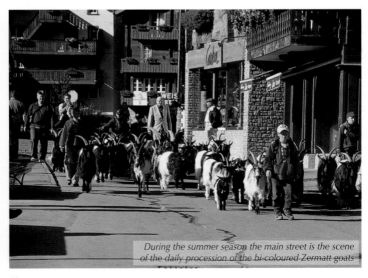

During the summer season the main street is the scene of the daily procession of the bi-coloured Zermatt goats

up to Zermatt, the Mattertal. Zermatt means 'towards the meadows' and the Matterhorn took its name accordingly. Previously it was known in German as the Hirschberg, meaning 'stag mountain'. The Italians and French know it as Monte Cervino and Le Cervin respectively. It is assumed that these names come from the word 'cerf', meaning stag. Another possibility is that the Italian and French names come from the Roman name; early descriptions of the Theodulpass speak of Mont Silvius, which is presumed to refer to the Matterhorn. The pass was known as Silvius in Roman times.

Why the Matterhorn is a part of Africa

Once again it was that endlessly curious soul, de Saussure, who initially suspected the geological origins of the Matterhorn. Around 90 million years ago the mountain did not exist. The African and Eurasian plates were kept apart by the Tethys Sea, which at that time separated Laurasia from Gondwanaland.

Slowly the African plate started to move closer to the Eurasian plate and a collision ensued. The pressure formed great folds (nappes) that rose out of the Tethys Sea and pushed northward, often breaking and sliding one over the other to form gigantic thrust faults, which became the peaks we see today. In the final stage of the Tethys Sea's disappearance (its remnants would form the Atlantic

Ocean), the large mass of African plate that was originally far to the south was pressed onto and over the deep ocean layers – basically, as Africa moved north, the European continent was squashed underneath it. Thus some mountains, including the Matterhorn, are formed from what was the African plate.

The first ascent

The imposing pyramid of the Matterhorn dominates Zermatt. It is interesting to wonder just how much this impacted on the early settlers to the valley. Did they ever consider that one day the summit would be climbed? Did they believe that bad spirits inhabited those lofty ridges, and that the summit was the source of ill fortune?

Certainly by the mid 19th century the first ascent of the Matterhorn was a much sought-after goal. This was the golden age of Alpinism and most of the major summits of the Alps had already fallen, often to British mountaineers accompanied by local Guides. The two main candidates were Jean Antoine Carrel from Breuil, and England's prodigious Alpinist Edward Whymper. Several attempts had been made on the summit, all resulting in retreat, but in mid July 1865 both men felt confident they could reach the summit. Whymper expected to undertake the climb accompanied by Carrel, but arriving in Breuil found that Carrel had already assembled his own team

The four ridges of the Matterhorn are all popular routes. From Zermatt the Normal Route is the Hörnli arête (seen here defined by light and shade)

and was en route. Hurrying back to Zermatt Whymper knew he could be pipped at the post if he didn't get moving. His choice of partners was limited to those who were free at that moment. Along with Michel Croz, his faithful Chamonix Guide, Whymper teamed up with a motley assortment of more or less experienced climbers: Lord Francis Douglas, Swiss Guides Peter Taugwalder and his son, Reverend Charles Hudson and Douglas Hadow. They set off immediately, keenly aware of Carrel's head start.

They took the northeast ridge of the mountain known as the Hörnli, and made quick progress. After a final steeper climb they succeeded in their quest, and looking down from the summit could see Carrel's team some way below on the Italian Ridge. Allegedly Whymper and team knocked rocks down to signify their presence, making sure there was no doubt they had got there first. Understandably Carrel was just a touch miffed and he gave up for the day, even though he had almost made the first ascent of the southwest ridge from Italy.

However, the Zermatt team had yet to get down. Slopes always look much steeper on descent, and the Hörnli ridge of the Matterhorn is no exception. Factor in the inexperience of some team members, the inevitable fatigue and perhaps lack of concentration following such a momentous ascent, and it's hardly surprising that Hadow slipped. The tragedy is that he took with him Croz, Hudson and

Douglas. The slender hemp rope, loaded well beyond its limit by the enormous impact of several bodies sliding into space, broke, leaving the Taugwalders and Whymper to descend to Zermatt to break the tragic news.

There followed a huge controversy, fuelled by the British press. *The Times*, for example, questioned, 'Is it life? Is it common sense? Is it duty? Is it allowable? Is it wrong?' Queen Victoria even enquired whether such a perilous sport could be banned by law.

Carrel climbed his Italian Ridge three days later. He went on to make 52 ascents of the peak, and died during a descent in bad weather in 1891, aged 62. Whymper erected a cross in his memory at the base of the Italian side of the Matterhorn.

For many years after Whymper and his team made their ascent rumours circulated that the rope between the four climbers who died and those who survived had been cut. The piece of rope can be seen in Zermatt museum. It seemed very unlikely that in the heat of the moment a climber could whip out a knife and slice the rope before being pulled off himself, and the theory was definitively disproved in 2005 after extensive studies of the rope.

Further ascents

The first female ascent was by Lucy Walker in 1871, in the company of Melchior Anderegg, her Guide from Zermatt. The first official winter

By the time the sun's first rays hit the East Face of the Matterhorn climbers should be well on the way up

ascent was made in March 1882 by the renowned Italian photographer and Alpinist, Vittorio Sella, with three Carrels, all Guides. The North Face was first climbed in 1931 by brothers Franz and Toni Schmid, and since then many hard routes have been added to the mountain. In addition the East Face is fairly regularly skied by those who can envisage such a feat.

Since the first ascent it is estimated that over 500 people have died whilst climbing the Matterhorn, which averages more than 12 deaths a year. In high season there can be more than 200 people on the mountain on one day. It is estimated that one in three candidates achieves his or her dream, to reach the summit and get down safely.

The Italian summit now sports a fine iron cross which was erected in the early 1900s. In 1902 the idea was proposed of putting crosses on major summits in honour of God. The Matterhorn cross weighs 85 kilos and it took three attempts before it was successfully carried up in pieces and blessed on the summit.

THE VALLEYS

A look at the different valleys crossed during the Tour of the Matterhorn gives an insight into the varied cultures of the region and the reason why, for centuries before the mountains were seen as anything other than a hindrance to survival – not a playground, as they are now – local people made the arduous, dangerous

On the Matterhorn summit

The 1991 landslide at Randa

journey across high passes from one valley to the other.

Mattertal

Legend has it that long ago, before the Alps were discovered by climbers and walkers – when mountains were still regarded as the abode of evil spirits and dragons – people believed that a magic valley lay hidden among the glaciers of Monte Rosa, amongst the big peaks. It is said that in 1788 a band of men set out from the Valle di Lys in Italy in search of this Eldorado. They climbed over the pass between Monte Rosa and Liskamm (now the Lysjoch) and looked down to the valley below. However, they were disappointed only to find more glaciers, rocks, snowfields, deep ravines. Where were the grassy meadows, milk and honey they had been looking for? Perhaps they would not be so disappointed now, seeing how the dawn of mountaineering and the consequent explosion in tourism has made this valley both a haven for holidaymakers and a most lucrative place for the inhabitants.

Interesting visits

- From Zermatt it is highly recommended that you take the time to walk the Höhbalmen. It is possible that after the Tour of the Matterhorn you'll be 'Matterhorned out', but give it a day or so then do this circuit for some of the best scenery possible. The route goes from Zermatt past Zmutt to the junction

with the path to the Schönbielhütte, which is also worth a visit. The Höhbalmen goes right where this path goes left, and up onto a high shelf from where the views not only of the Matterhorn but also of the Mischabel and Mont Rosa peaks are fantastic. On the descent be sure to stop at Trift to sample their home-made iced tea. If you have time spend the night here in the company of owners Hugo and Fabienne – you will not find a warmer and more informed host than Hugo, who is also a UIAGM Guide.

- Many people like to walk up to the Hörnlihütte to see where people start the Matterhorn climb, and if you go just a little way beyond the hut you can touch the rock of the summit.

- The Gornergrat railway provides an easy way to view the summits. This train goes up to 3000m, a very pleasant outing for a rest day. From here the views of the Gorner Glacier and surrounding peaks are breathtaking.

- Those who enjoy skiing might be tempted by a day's activity from the Klein Matterhorn lift.

Turtmanntal

This is the wildest valley encountered, relatively undeveloped and with summer-only road access. It is a haven for wildlife, ranging from chamois to lynx to eagles, and in 1946 the last Swiss wolf was killed here.

Interesting visits

Given the time a walk up to the Turtmannhütte would be fun for the views of the peaks and the Brunnegg and Turtmann glaciers.

Val d'Anniviers

The Val d'Anniviers has been called 'The finest valley on the Swiss side of the Pennine Alps' (J.H. Walker, *Walking in the Alps*). This is a valley of wonderful old villages and it would be easy to spend days here discovering the charms of St Luc, Grimentz and Vissoie, as well as Zinal which is actually on our route. The Val d'Anniviers has a friendly and cultivated air – a step back in time certainly, but not a step into the wilds. For many years the Anniviard people regularly made the journey from the Rhône Valley up to their summer villages.

The head of the valley is overlooked by huge summits such as the Zinal Rothorn and the Weisshorn.

Interesting visits

- The Cabane de Mountet makes a good day walk from Zinal, and is definitely worth the effort for the splendid views of the Weisshorn and the Glacier de Moming.
- The village of Grimentz, which can be reached by bus from Zinal, is a real gem, one of the most beautiful traditional Alpine villages around. For a rest day this would provide plenty of interest for those who enjoy looking at old chalets and eating ice-cream in the sunshine.

- There is an interesting walk to the Hotel Weisshorn, the Chemin Planetaire, which has as its theme the solar planets. It has been set up by the François-Xavier Bagnoud Observatory at Tignousa above St Luc. At intervals along the path are models of the planets placed proportionately at their true distance from the sun, which is situated at the start of the walk at Tignousa.
- Above the Moiry Lake the Cabane de Moiry gives fine views of the Moiry Glacier and associated summits.

Val d'Hérens

The Hérens Valley is famous for its cows (see Hérens Cows, p123), and farming predominates here. The valley is bordered by meadows filled with flowers in the summer, scattered with summer chalets and stables. The Dent Blanche guards the end of the valley, towering over Les Haudères.

Interesting visits

- Take the bus down the valley towards Sion. The amazing Pyramides Euseignes are caused by erosion of the relatively soft hillsides which has caused harder boulders to become stranded, balanced on the tops of these pyramids. Definitely worth a look.
- Towards Arolla, the Lac Bleu can be reached in an hour from the road (access by bus from Les Haudères) – quite a sight with its incredibly blue waters.

Above the Moiry valley formed by the Moiry Glacier and its high peaks (Stage 4)

- If you're staying in Arolla with a spare day, hike up to the Pas de Chèvres. This gives access to the Dix Glacier and hut. The ladder down from the pass is quite impressive, and the views of Mont Blanc de Cheilon, Pigne d'Arolla and Mont Collon are stunning.

Valpelline

A far more severe mountain environment is to be found here, with many of the summits and passes rarely being climbed.

Interesting visits

- A rest day could be spent taking the bus down to Chatillon then to Aosta. This Roman town still has many Roman monuments, and a day can easily be spent enjoying the sites and the Valdotain specialities. If you take the Pila cable car you get a spectacular panorama of the Alps, from Mont Blanc to the Matterhorn to Monte Rosa to the Gran Paradiso peaks.
- There are many castles to be visited in the Aosta Valley, and guides (in English) are available from the tourist office.
- There are various summer festivals: the last Sunday in July sees the Festival of the Seuppa à la Vapelenentze, a gastronomic speciality of black bread, soup and fontina cheese; on the first Sunday of August at St Oyen there is a ham celebration; August is also the month of the Fontina festival in Oyace, giving a chance to taste the famous local cheese.

The Pyramides Euseignes in the Val d'Hérens are an unusual sight

- From Valpelline it is not too far to visit the Grand St Bernard Pass, home of monks and dogs.
- The Valpelline Visitors Centre offers guided tours and shopping; tel: 0165.73309 www.fontinacoop.com

Valtournanche

This is the Italian valley dominated by the Matterhorn (or rather Monte Cervino). This valley really represents the Valle d'Aosta and its first language traditionally was French, hence the name Breuil, which it has held onto albeit joined to the name Cervinia, given by Mussolini for political reasons.

Interesting visits

- There is a bus service to Chatillon, then onwards north or south in the main Aosta Valley. Those interested in wine could spend an interesting day checking out some of the vineyards where wine tasting is possible.
- If you have transport the St Barthélemy Valley makes a delightful drive, and you could include a visit to the astronomy centre at Lignan.
- The Gouffre des Busserailles on the road to Breuil-Cervinia, 3km before Valtournenche. Before entering the gorge you can see the *marmitte dei giganti*, so-called because of their imposing cauldron shape. A bit further on you can see the ravine, a fissure in the rock dating from the Ice Age, shaped by the water and the glaciers of the Matterhorn which in far-off times submerged the valley. Going on, there is a 35m-high waterfall.

On a sunny day the village of Gruben Meiden is Paradise (Stage 2)

- St Vincent, down in the main valley, is famous for its thermal baths, open from May to October. There are also Roman ruins under the church of Saint-Vincent and along the traces of the imperial road to Gaul. The present parish church, one of the most ancient in the Aosta Valley, was built on an area of previous late Gallic buildings and Roman baths. In the parish museum there are woodcarvings, frescos and fresco cartoons.
- A visit to Aosta is highly recommended, as suggested for the Valpelline visits above.

4000m SUMMITS

On the Tour of the Matterhorn you will see more than 25 summits which surpass the magical height of 4000m.

This height is considered important in the Alps in much the same way as 8000m is regarded as a milestone in the Himalayas. There are officially 61 summits in the Alps over 4000m and there are people who 'bag' the peaks, just as in the USA the Colorado 14,000ft peaks are sought after. In Britain hikers lust after the 'Munros' – peaks in Scotland over 3000ft.

Whether you're a peak bagger or not it's interesting to know a little more about the major peaks likely to draw your gaze during the trek.

Dom 4545m

This is the highest peak set entirely in Switzerland, and it stands proud on the east side of the Mattertal – it is one of the peaks forming a backdrop for the stage from Jungu to

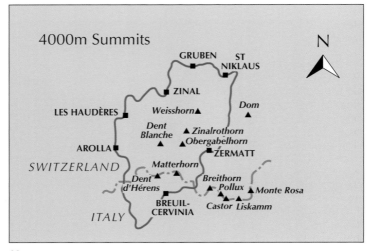

The Dom provides a straightforward – if long – glacier hike

the Augstbordpass. Its name has variously been reported either to come from that of Canon (Domherr) Berchthold, the first to survey the Valais canton, or to have been given by him and to mean 'Deo Optimo Maximo' (God is good and big). Whichever version is true, there's no doubt that the Dom has a size and magnificence that reach heavenly proportions. Nevertheless its ascent by the North Face presents no real difficulties, being a huge glaciated slope which is popular summer and winter alike as the Normal Route up the mountain. It was first ascended in 1858 by Rev J.L. Davies, with Guides J. Zum Taugwald, J. Kronig and J. Schwarzen. They left Randa at 2am, reached the summit at 11am, and returned to Randa at 4.20pm to then walk up to Zermatt for dinner.

However, not everyone seems enamoured with this route: in his book *The Alpine 4000m Peaks* Richard Goedeke describes it as 'a miserable snow-plod, but on account of the overwhelming monotony of its enormous dimensions still an impressive undertaking'.

Dent Blanche 4356m

Logically this huge summit, a veritable fortress of gneiss, should be named the Dent d'Hérens, but a mix-up (see Dent d'Hérens below) ended up with the names being reversed. This is the highest summit in Swiss Romande and it has seen its fair share of accidents, particularly towards the

Looking up the valley towards Zinal, with the Dent Blanche on the left (Stage 3)

late 19th century. It forms almost the perfect pyramid with four beautiful arêtes. It was first ascended in 1862 by Britons T.S. Kennedy and W. Wigram, with Guides J. Kronig and J.B. Croz, by the south ridge. The east ridge, which sports the name 'Arête des 4 ânes' (Arête of the 4 asses) was named in self-derision by the first ascentionists.

The Dent Blanche dominates the head of the Hérens Valley and is seen to great advantage from the balcony trail leading to Zinal. In fact the Dent Blanche has its roots in three valleys – the Hérens, the Val d'Anniviers and the Mattertal. Great views of it are to be had from the Matterhorn. In the past the Zermatt people called it the Steinbockhorn – the Ibex peak.

Dent d'Hérens 4171m

This peak stands right next to Matterhorn, and although a little upstaged by its famous neighbour the Dent d'Hérens nevertheless presents its own formidable challenges. It is quite remote, being at the far end of the Mattertal and equally far from the valleys in Italy. It is a mountain of steep faces and elegant arêtes. The name 'Dent d'Hérens' is a misnomer as this name was originally given to what is now the Dent Blanche at the head of the Val d'Hérens. In a mistake made on the 19th-century maps the names got reversed, and have stuck ever since.

The Dent d'Hérens is seen during the climb up to the Col Collon, and from Breuil-Cervinia next to the Matterhorn.

Liskamm 4527m

Liskamm can boast a mighty 5km-long ridge, a dubious claim to fame as this arête is notorious for its cornices (often double-sided), and a traverse of the mountain is only for those with stable feet and steady nerves. It has two summits, the east of which rises 50m higher than the west, which is about a kilometre away. Its original name of Silberbast ('silver saddle' in local dialect) would therefore seem appropriate.

The peak was first ascended in 1861, the 1860s being a time of great activity in these mountains. The first ascent party was a huge team of six Swiss Guides and eight British clients

and they took a route up the southeast ridge. The peak was first traversed by Guides J. Anderegg and F. Biner with L. Stephen and E. Buxton in 1864. The first disaster on the mountain occurred in 1877 when a party fell to their deaths when a cornice broke. This was the start of this mountain's dark history, leading to the reputation it has today. As Oscar Erich Meyer put it, those who have died 'did not die at its foot, on its walls or on its ridges, but were cast from the crest into the depths. All at once, all whom the rope had bound together. For thus are cornices. Day after day the wind kneads and shapes them… and it is man who, in deadly bond with his

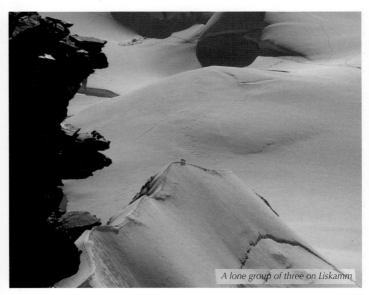

A lone group of three on Liskamm

From left to right: Monte Rosa, Liskamm, Castor, Pollux and the Breithorn

companions, tips the scales. Thus the Liskamm kills. It gives no warnings, it strikes like lightning.'

So, probably a peak best enjoyed from afar – you'll get good views of it if you climb the Breithorn, and more distantly from the viewpoint above Jungu on Stage 2.

Zinal Rothorn 4221m

One of the only 4000m peaks visible from the Rhône Valley, notably from Sierre, this summit dominates the Anniviers Valley. It has its roots equally in the Mattertal and the Val d'Anniviers, but obviously was named by the people of Zinal (although it was originally known in local patois

as the 'Moming'). It is very much a rock peak, formed of gneiss, pyramidal in form, with three excellent rocky ridges, the best being the particularly fine southwest ridge (the Rothorngrat) which – for quality of climbing and rock – is one of the best ridges in the Alps.

Melchoir Anderegg, one of the Guides on the first ascent by the north ridge, declared that the Rothorn was one of the few peaks where the Guide could barely look after his client.

Like other neighbouring peaks there are no lifts to assist with access, and to ascend it you must approach from the valley on foot – although, for a price, Air Zermatt will drop you off above the Rothornhütte.

It was on this summit that early female mountaineer Mrs Aubrey Le Blond inadvertently left her skirt. Realising her mistake as she neared the valley, she had to go all the way back to get it. No skirt was not an option for 19th-century ladies.

The Zinal Rothorn will provide a great backdrop for your photos at several points on the Tour of the Matterhorn. You will see it when arriving in the Val d'Anniviers, en route over to Moiry, and of course from the Theodulpass and the descent to Zermatt.

Obergabelhorn 4063m

Situated next to the Zinal Rothorn, this is another peak of breathtaking beauty and elegance. It is a symmetrical four-sided pyramid whose South Face is sunny and whose North Face is appropriately icy and foreboding. Again a summit with no easy route – the Normal Route by the northeast ridge is steep, although fixed ropes on the gendarme make it easier than it was for the first ascent in 1890.

The summit was first reached in 1865 by A.W. Moore, H. Walker and J. Anderegg, who climbed the East Face. The next day Lord Francis Douglas reached the top by the northwest ridge on his third attempt, this having been his dream for sometime. Douglas climbed to the highest point of the mountain, noticing that there were no fresh footprints up there from the day

before (in fact Moore had noted that the top would be dangerous, so had stopped just below). Whilst he was having lunch the top collapsed, and luckily he was held by the rope to his fellow climbers. Two weeks later he was less fortunate when he climbed the Matterhorn as part of the first ascent team, and the rope did not hold.

Strangely, when I did the Obergabelhorn with my husband we found fresh fox tracks on the summit.

Weisshorn 4505m

The Weisshorn is the second-highest summit solely in Switzerland, and was apparently named by the people of St Niklaus for the luminosity of its North Face. It was first ascended by Irishman John Tyndall in 1861, with Guides J.J. Bennen and U. Wenger. Tyndall was a contender for the first ascent of the Matterhorn, and one of the ridge pinnacles on that peak is named after him. He achieved fame for discovering that the sky is blue because of the diffusion of light.

There are no easy routes up the Weisshorn, and you will come to know its North and East Face well if you choose to walk the Europaweg from Zermatt to Grächen. The beauty and purity of this pyramidal summit has made the Weisshorn one of the most sought-after 4000m peaks in the Alps. The mountain has extra kudos as there is no road or lift to help reduce the ascent; even the Normal Route, the east ridge, requires a long ascent from and descent to the valley.

Monte Rosa (on the left) has the biggest mass of any range in the western Alps

Once again Richard Goedeke doesn't exactly sell the idea: '...a wretched 1500m hut walk'!

Castor 4228m/Pollux 4092m

Named either after the sons of the Goddess Leda, heroes of Greek mythology, or a constellation, these are the Zwillinge (twins), seen as two small summits, surrounded as they are by giants. They are between the huge mountain masses of the Breithorn and Liskamm. Castor is the southeasterly and higher twin and appears as a rounded white summit, whereas Pollux is rockier. These peaks are often climbed together in a day, in winter and summer, and can be incorporated into a multi-day glaciated traverse of the Zermatt frontier peaks.

They are easy to identify when you have views of the whole range from the Breithorn to Liskamm, such as from above Jungu. They are also, of course, visible from the Breithorn and the descent to Zermatt.

Monte Rosa 4634m

The Monte Rosa massif is a group of 10 summits, all over 4000m, the highest of which is the Dufourspitze (4634m). It is a mountain range of superlatives: it is the most enormous mountain massif in the Alps (Mont Blanc attains a higher altitude, but doesn't get anywhere near in terms of mountain mass); it covers 500km² and has 140km² of glaciers; it straddles the Swiss–Italian frontier; the East Face of Monte Rosa seen from Macugnaga is the highest face in the Alps (2600m, and has been compared to a Himalayan face); the Gorner Glacier, which flows down to the Mattertal, is 14km long; and the Rifugio Margerita on the summit of Signalkuppe (4554m) takes the prize for highest hut in Europe.

Leonardo Da Vinci declared that 'no other mountain lies at such a height', and certainly if we're talking massifs this is the highest in western Europe. Documents in Zermatt record Winston Churchill's ascent of the Dufourspitze in 1884.

FLOWERS AND VEGETATION

The flora encountered during any trek depends on the time of year. Even though an Alpine trek of this nature can only really be done as a regular walk during the summer months there is a huge change in vegetation between late June and late September. Early on in the summer season the lower slopes around the villages will be a blaze of colour as all the meadow flowers are in bloom up to around 2000m – trumpet gentians, pasque flowers, alpenrose, vetch, martagon lilies... a perfect time to be walking at the lower altitudes. However, higher up there may still be névé remaining from the winter, and since most slopes will only just be snowfree the flowers will not yet be out.

As the summer progresses many of the lower meadows will be scythed for hay, but above 2000m the flowers will begin to bloom. Again the alpenrose is prevalent. A member of the Azalea family, this bush covers the slopes from about 1500–2500m. Its pink flowers make a wonderful backdrop for hiking, and to trek in the Alps when it is in bloom is an absolute joy. You will also find all manner of flowers that may be seen at lower altitudes, but higher up they will be smaller and often more intense in colour. The houseleeks that grow on the rocks, astrantia and orange hawksbeard are all Alpine versions of regular garden flowers. Above 2500–3000m we

The houseleek and friend

The colourful alpine toadflax can be seen on high barren slopes

Rosehips are a sure sign that summer is giving way to autumn

find the real Alpine gems, those tiny jewel-like flowers, so small they get lost in rocky crevices. These flowers only have about a six-week growing season, so have to be very efficient to grow and polinate before the snows return. Hence their miniature size to save energy, and bright colours to maximise their attraction to insects. Look out for starry blue gentians and clumps of pink rock jasmine on the high rocky passes, as well as the rare king of the Alps which you may be lucky to spot on a couple of the cols. Scree slopes are often home to the amazing purple and orange toadflax, whilst the highest ground is where you'll find the pinky white buttercup-like flowers of the glacier crowsfoot, allegedly the flower that grows at the highest altitude in the Alps.

Of course the flower everyone expects to see is the edelweiss and you should be lucky somewhere along this trek, providing you are not too early – the flowers do not generally bloom before mid July. Don't be too surprised when you do find it – why the edelweiss has become the classic Alpine flower can only be guessed at – its white furry bracts can appear rather grey. But look closely and you'll see that in fact the real flower is the yellow centre – seen in sunlight it is rather fine. If you trek in September a keen eye will still spot many different species at higher altitudes. Lower down will be a few late-season blooms such as purple monkshood, growing next to streams, or the Alpine pansy that seems to keep going for the whole summer. Also as summer progresses you'll find the lower paths bordered by bilberry bushes, laden with berries, and raspberries too, the lure of which makes for slow progress at times. There are also some low-lying bushes bearing shiny red berries, bear berries, which are used to make a savoury jelly.

There is also a wide variety of trees, depending on altitude. The Alps are known for their coniferous forests, largely composed of spruce and pine. These forests are brightened up by the presence of larch trees, the only deciduous conifer. Their needles are a pleasant light green in the spring and turn golden before falling in the autumn. The larch is one of the best woods for construction, and most old chalets are made at least in part from this beautiful red wood.

A tree peculiar to the Alps is the Arolla pine, which has long needles and is often seen on the limit of the treeline – the higher up it grows, the smaller and more stunted it is. This extremely hardy tree can resist temperatures as low as minus 50°C, and is indifferent to soil quality or aspect of the slope. Its wood is one of the most sought after, especially by sculptors. Its cones are sturdy, and the seeds too heavy to be blown by the wind. Instead these seeds are eaten, notably by the nuthatch, which tends to store the seeds in cracks in rocks. Hence the Arolla pine is classically found growing out from the most improbable boulders.

WILDLIFE

One of the highlights of walking in the mountains is the chance of seeing the local wildlife. In the Alps there is a whole host of animals and birds that you may be lucky enough to see along the trail. The chamois, ibex and

A lone ibex near Rifugio Perrucca-Vuillermoz (Stage 6)

Chamois are generally quite timid, and will take off when they see or hear you coming

marmot are the three 'must sees', but plenty of other animals inhabit these mountain valleys, meadows and boulderfields. In the forests there are several types of deer, generally seen early in the morning or at dusk. Wild boar live below about 1500m, and their snuffling antics often leave the edge of the footpaths churned up. The chewed pinecones lying on the trail attest to the presence of squirrels, which you will probably spot nipping from tree to tree.

If you are first on the trail you have the best chance of a wildlife sighting. Don't make too much noise, or they will certainly clock you first. The meadows and rocks are home to the mountain hare which is very timid and more often seen in winter – at least its tracks are – and the stoat, which

scampers around rocks, always curious but very fast. They say there are lynx in the Alps but they are either very rare or very cautious, and to see one would be quite a surprise.

There is also plentiful birdlife, ranging from the very small to the very, very big. Any forest walk will be accompanied by the happy chirping of tits, finches and goldcrests, and the drilling noises of busy woodpeckers. Buzzards are common at the lower levels, and higher up golden eagles are not rare – especially on bad weather days when they circle high above on the air currents. On the high cols you will be joined by Alpine choughs the moment you get out your butties. These black birds, recognisable by their yellow beaks, live as high as 8000m in the

Himalayas. But the king of them all has to be the lammergeier, or bearded vulture, reintroduced throughout the Alps over the last few years. You will be lucky to see one, but if you spot a huge bird with an orange underbelly that only seems to flap once an hour then the chances are it's a lammergeier. These giants, long regarded as meat-eating predators, actually live almost entirely off the bones of dead animals. They drop the bones from height to break them up for easier consumption; very occasionally you may see a heap of broken bones lying near the trail.

It is a great privilege to see these creatures. Whilst taking photographs is a superb way to immortalise the moment, it is crucial to leave them undisturbed. There's nothing so ridiculous as watching a would-be photographer stalking his subject while the animal moves further and further away. Fit your camera with a strong zoom lens, or be satisfied to keep the memory in your head.

THINGS TO DO AND SEE

There are countless specialities to look out for, too numerous to list. One of the joys of a trek is discovering the local traditions for yourself. However, here are just a few things you must not miss.

Hugo, his alpenhorn and the Hotel du Trift above Zermatt

In Italy

Anything from the Valle d'Aosta takes the adjective 'Valdôtain' or 'Valdostain'.

La Fontina is the classic Valle d'Aosta cheese. The grazing meadows of the Aosta Valley are situated at altitude, often above 2500m. This cheese can be traced back many centuries; it is portrayed in frescoes in some of the many castles in the area, and documented in tracts as far back as the 13th century. The cheese became legendary in the 19th century thanks to the praise heaped on it by European travellers. In the Valpelline, source of much of the Fontina, thousands of cheeses are kept in an old copper mine, the largest reserve in the Aosta Valley.

Wine There is a huge tradition of viticulture in the Aosta Valley. Frescoes from early times depict vines as being essential to everyday life. Not only did wine make life more bearable for the average peasant, it also constituted a means of paying dues to the lords and notables of the region. The Valdôtain wines were also exported to neighbouring valleys. The sunny slopes above the Dora Baltea river which runs along the valley provide perfect terrain for vineyards. Several wines are peculiar to the region, and wine tends to be produced communally in co-operatives.

Wood carving Everywhere you go in the valley you'll see intricate carvings, often depicting scenes from daily life. These range from kitchen implements and decorative plates to full-scale furniture and doors.

In Switzerland

The Valais region (Wallis in German-speaking Switzerland) is a bigger and less compact area than the Valle d'Aosta. The culture is already diluted by two languages, but nevertheless there are some specialities to look out for.

Switzerland is, of course, known for its **chocolate**, and wherever you go you'll find samples of varying quality.

Cheese is also produced throughout the region. Fondue is the classic dish, made with white wine and served with cubes of bread. However, there are variations on this theme, one of the best being tomato fondue, a cheese and tomato sauce served on mashed potato. The other dish not to miss is **rösti,** essentially a plate of grated and fried potato, garnished with egg, ham, bacon…This is served especially around Zermatt, where all the huts and mountain restaurants have it on the menu – it will always be good.

If you are lucky you may come across people playing the **Alpenhorn**, a very long wooden horn traditional to the Swiss Alps. The sound is haunting, and if played in a mountain combe it can echo right across the slopes.

If you are on the Swiss part of the trek on 1 August prepare to party as this is **Swiss National Day** and all the towns and villages will have festivals.

Descending the Comba d'Oren (Stage 5)

SHORTER TREKKING ALTERNATIVES

There are lots of possibilities for doing a part of the Tour of the Matterhorn. Try the following suggestions:

Arolla to Zermatt

This part of the tour can be done in four days and is a good option if you have already done (or plan to do) the Tour of Monte Rosa and the Chamonix–Zermatt Walker's Route. A suggested itinerary would be:

1 Arolla to Prarayer
2 Prarayer to Rifugio Perucca-Vuillermoz
3 Rifugio Perucca-Vuillermoz to Theodulehütte
4 Theodulehütte to Zermatt.

Tour of the Matterhorn – Swiss side

You could divide the Tour of the Matterhorn into two separate treks: Swiss and Italian. The Swiss one would be non-glaciated and could begin in Zermatt. You could do the Europaweg, then go on over the Val d'Anniviers to the Val d'Hérens. A suggested itinerary would be:

1 Zermatt to the Europahütte
2 Europahütte to St Niklaus
3 St Niklaus to Gruben-Meiden
4 Gruben-Meiden to Zinal
5 Zinal to Moiry
6 Moiry to Les Haudères
7 Les Haudères to Arolla
8 Arolla to Pas de Chèvres: day walk for a last glimpse of the Matterhorn if you have good weather.

Tour of the Matterhorn – Italian side

This would include the ascent of the Breithorn and could be started and finished in Italy. A suggested itinerary would be:

1 Bus from Aosta to Valpelline, then taxi to Place Moulin; walk to Rifugio Prarayer
2 Rifugio Prarayer to Rifugio Perucca-Vuillermoz
3 Rifugio Perucca-Vuillermoz to Theodulehütte
4 Ascent of Breithorn, then descent to Breuil-Cervinia and bus to Aosta.

Glacier route variant

There is a four-day variant Tour of the Matterhorn as follows:

Day 1   Zermatt to Schönbielhütte (2694m)
Day 2   Tête de Valpelline (3798m) to Col de la Division to Rifugio Aosta to Rifugio Prarayer
Day 3   Colle di Bella Tza (3047m) to Rifugio Perucca to Vuillermoz
Day 4   As for the regular tour to Breuil-Cervinia.

Good walks from Zermatt include

- The Mettlehorn summit, which is accessed from Trift.
- The circuit from Sunegga to Riflealp to Gornergrat.
- The villages of Winkelmatten and Findeln, then on up to Grindjsee and Sunegga.

Good walks from Breuil-Cervinia include

- The Colle Supérieur delle Cime Bianche from Plan Maison.
- The Rifugio Duca Degli Abruzzi for its proximity to the Matterhorn.

THE TREK

Route Outline

Stage 1 **Zermatt to St Niklaus**
Main version Zermatt – Sunnegga (by footpath or lift) – Tufteren – Täschalp – Europahütte – Gasenried – Grächen – St Niklaus
Alternative valley route Zermatt – Täsch – Randa – Breimattern – Herbriggen – St Niklaus

Distance	**36**	Time	**12.5**
Ascent	**1060**	Descent	**1580**

Stage 2 **St Niklaus to Gruben-Meiden**
St Niklaus – Jungu (either cable car or footpath) – ridge of Troara – Augstbordpass – Oberstafel – Mittelstafel – Gruben-Meiden

Distance	**12**	Time	**8**
Ascent	**1790**	Descent	**1075**

Stage 3 **Gruben-Meiden to Zinal**
Gruben-Meiden – Meide – Meidpass – La Roja – Hotel Weisshorn Bella Lé – junction to Forcletta – Barneuxa – Zinal
Option Forcletta Pass

Distance	**19**	Time	**8**
Ascent	**965**	Descent	**1140**

Stage 4 **Zinal to Les Haudères**
Zinal – Sorebois (cable car or footpath) – Col de Sorebois – Lac de Moiry – Lac des Autannes – Col de Torrent – Villa – La Sage – Les Haudères

Distance	**22**	Time	**11**
Ascent	**1975**	Descent	**2180**

Link stage **Les Haudères to Arolla**

Distance	**15**	Time	**3**
Ascent	**585**	Descent	**85**

Stage 5 **Arolla to Prarayer**
Arolla – Haut Glacier d'Arolla – La Vierge – Col Collon – Rifugio Collon-Nacamuli – Prarayer

Distance	**17**	Time	**9**
Ascent	**1080**	Descent	**1085**

Stage 6   **Prararyer to Breuil-Cervinia**
Prararyer – Alp Valcournera – Colle di Valcournera – Rifugio
Perrucca-Vuillermoz – Alpe di Cignana – Finestra di Cignana –
Perrères – Breuil-Cervinia

Distance	**14**	Time	**9**
Ascent	**1080**	Descent	**1060**

Stage 7   **Breuil-Cervinia to Zermatt**
Breuil-Cervinia – Plan Maison – Theodulpass – Theodulehütte –
Gandegghütte – Trocknersteg – Furi – Zermatt

Distance	**19**	Time	**9.5**
Ascent	**1290**	Descent	**1720**

TOTALS	Distance	**145km**	Time	**70hrs**
	Ascent	**9925m**	Descent	**9925m**

The pond near Beplan after the Col de Torrent (Stage 4)

STAGE 1
Zermatt to St Niklaus

Start	Zermatt
Access to start	Train from Visp; bus and road access to Täsch; train to Zermatt.
Altitude at start	1600m
Finish	St Niklaus
Access to finish	Train from Visp; train from Zermatt; bus from Visp; bus from Grächen; road access.
Altitude at finish	1120m
Altitude gain	1160m
Altitude loss	1680m
Distance	36km
Time	12+hrs. Zermatt to Europahütte: 6hrs 30mins; Europahütte to St Niklaus: 6hrs.
Highpoint	2663m on Europaweg soon after Galen Berg, before descent to Grächen.
Maps	1:50,000 Carte Nationale de la Suisse 5006 Matterhorn Mischabel; 1:25,000 Carte Nationale de la Suisse 1328 Randa, 1308 St Niklaus
Facilities	Zermatt has every facility under the sun; Täschalp has a café, no shops; Grächen has shops and ATMs, as does St Niklaus.
Transport options	Sunegga lift out of Zermatt; bus from Grächen to St Niklaus.
Accommodation	Zermatt: lots of hotels; Täsch, Randa: hotels; Täschalp: Europaweghütte; Europahütte; Grächen: several hotels; St Niklaus: several hotels.
Extras	If there has been a lot of rain recently it's worth checking that the Europaweg is practicable as it is prone to landslides and rockfall. If in doubt take the valley route described below.
Escape route	There are several paths down to the valley from the Europaweg to reach Täsch, Randa or Herbriggen, from where the train can be taken back to Zermatt.

For this stage there are two options: the Europaweg and the valley route. I have chosen to describe the former as the main route, and include directions for the valley route too.

The Europaweg is a relatively new path, which has been created by following some pre-existing paths and linking them together with new paths where necessary. It takes a high-level traverse all the way from Zermatt to Grächen, the small town situated high above the Mattertal just before the junction with the Saastal. From here the Europaweg links up with a much older balcony path known as the Höhenweg, which goes around to Saas Fee. This is the route taken by the Tour of Monte Rosa.

This balcony route provides a visual extravaganza as it keeps high above the Mattertal, giving unsurpassed views of the surrounding glaciated peaks. Star of the show is the Weisshorn, whose elegant east ridge and sculpted snowy North Face will time and again draw your gaze. There is something very satisfying about following such a path and knowing that for two days you need not descend to the valley, and there are countless wonderful vantage points that beckon the hiker to put down his sac and just stop and stare. If you get good weather for this stage then savour it – it is a unique experience.

The Europaweg from Zermatt to St Niklaus can be done in two or three days. For the two-day option – unless you're looking for a real stamina test – it is advisable to take the bus down from Grächen and maybe also use the Sunnegga lift out of Zermatt. Don't underestimate how tiring a traverse can be – it's certainly not flat and, as is often the case, the relatively small ascents feel much harder than they are as they disrupt the rhythm of the walk. Be prepared for an energetic hike and then you'll fully enjoy the pleasures of this amazing route.

For amazing it is, not only for the fine mountain views, but also for its audacious route across some clearly unstable slopes. Because of the constantly changing nature of the ground crossed the path makers have had to re-route the trail through tunnels made of corrugated metal. These feature at points on the path where rockfall is frequent, so you nip inside and emerge unscathed further along the slope. Nevertheless there are sections where signs advise you not to stop until you reach the next sign. All in all I think the inventors of the Europaweg have created a monster which will require endless maintenance but, for as long as they do that, it's a great route for good weather days.

There are two huts providing convenient accommodation along the route. The first is the Europaweghütte, a hut and café at Ottavan/Täschalp, and this would be a good stopover if you want to take three days on the route.

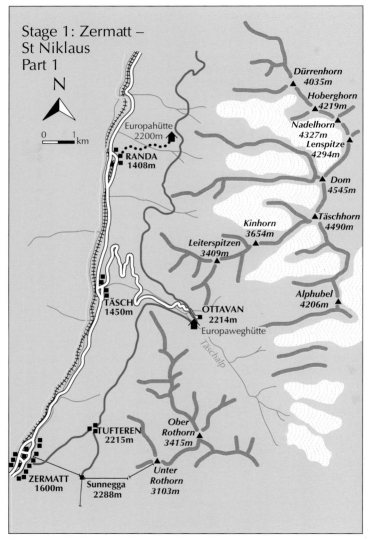

Stage 1: Zermatt –
St Niklaus
Part 1

N

0 — 1 km

Europahütte
2200m

RANDA
1408m

Dürrenhorn
4035m

Hoberghorn
4219m

Nadelhorn
4327m

Lenspitze
4294m

Dom
4545m

Kinhorn
3654m

Täschhorn
4490m

Leiterspitzen
3409m

Alphubel
4206m

TÄSCH
1450m

OTTAVAN
2214m
Europaweghütte

Täschalp

TUFTEREN
2215m

Ober
Rothorn
3415m

ZERMATT
1600m

Sunnegga
2288m

Unter
Rothorn
3103m

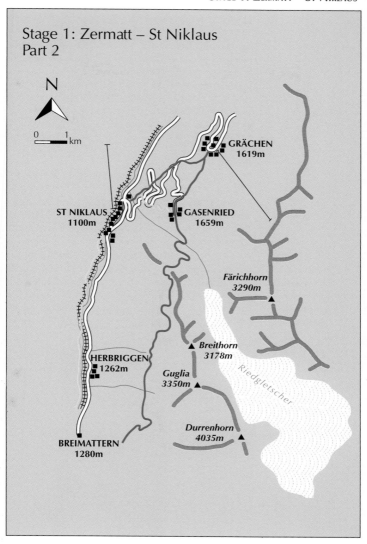

Stage 1: Zermatt – St Niklaus
Part 2

N

0 ____ 1 km

GRÄCHEN
1619m

ST NIKLAUS
1100m

GASENRIED
1659m

Färichhorn
3290m

HERBRIGGEN
1262m

Breithorn
3178m

Guglia
3350m

Riedgletscher

Durrenhorn
4035m

BREIMATTERN
1280m

However, most people will do the stage in two days and stay at the Europahütte, situated about halfway between Zermatt and Grächen. It is a beautiful wooden chalet perched high above the valley with amazing views of the Weisshorn, and is just after the junction with the path going up to the Domhütte. I am told the Europahütte can be very busy in the high season – there are tales of people sleeping on the tables and others being turned away. So prior reservation here would seem to be essential, as far in advance as possible.

Route

To reach **Sunnegga** from Zermatt go to the church and then across the river. Take the back roads that are signed Sunnegga, going up past Tiefenmatten and Patrullarve where there is a winter lift station. You will arrive at **Tufteren** (2215m) on a track by some pretty houses. (If taking the Sunnegga lift come out of the lift. There is a gondola lift which takes off from just below the lift station. Walk under this and look down to an obvious flat track with a signpost. Go down to this and Tufteren is signposted right. Go along this pleasant track which is flat and bordered by larch and spruce. It soon reaches the hamlet of Tufteren.)

The Europaweg will not be found on maps dating before 1998, when it was inaugurated.

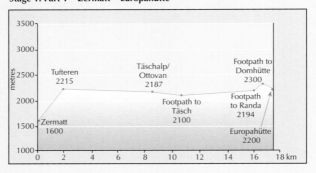

Stage 1: Part 1 – Zermatt – Europahütte

82

The Europaweg is signposted at a junction just above the buildings of Tufteren. The path rises gently then flattens out, heading around the hillside. There are several junctions but the Europaweg or the Europahütte are generally indicated. On this early part of the walk the other landmark to look out for is **Ottavan/Täschalp**. You should have good views of Obergabelhorn and Rothorn.

The path descends a little to continue its way around towards the hillside. Ahead a landslide can be seen down a slope. This is typical of what happens to the hillside on this walk. Many slopes are raked by avalanche and when they are the path gets wiped out. Landslides are also relatively common in heavy rain. This landslide is the other side of the deep valley which cuts into the hillside up to Ottavan/Täschalp and our path turns the corner and undulates along towards this hamlet. ▶

Ottavan/Täschalp is a lovely place to enjoy lunch, and if you have decided to take three days over this stage spend your frst night here (9km/3hrs).

Once there, the trail hits the road for a short while before a signed path off on the right is taken – marked as 3hr20 to Europahütte. This briefly goes uphill before once again traversing around with good views of the Matterhorn on left. It is at times exposed but there are always cables on the exposed parts. There is a section of descent with ropes on both sides and then long traverses

Stage 1: Part 2 – Europahütte – St Niklaus

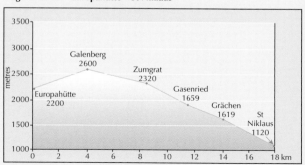

The Europaweg goes through several tunnels to avoid potential rockfall

protected where necessary. A river is crossed and it is clear that the path has to be re-made regularly, each time at a lower level. There is a series of tunnels on the trail interspersed with platforms to protect walkers from rockfall on the exposed slopes. One slope features four tunnels which must have been a huge amount of work to construct.

After a bouldery section and while climbing on a trail through boulders in the woods be careful not to miss a right hand switchback. Clearly lots of people have missed it because initially the way on (which is wrong) looks quite worn. The switchbacks lead to a junction where there is a path down to Randa.

Eventually a deep ravine is crossed by a bridge, followed by a roped section before another tunnel, this time cut into the rock. Look for the light switch on the right at the entrance (in typical Swiss fashion this is solar powered). After this you can see the Europahütte and it feels as if you're nearly there. However, soon after there is a misleading signpost. The upper path is signed to Gruen Garten, the middle path to the Europaweg and the lower path to Randa, but there is no lower path. It feels wrong to follow the lower of the two options as this descends, but it is correct. (The higher path may have previously led to the Europahütte but its continuation has been destroyed by erosion.) Not far down the lower path there is a sign left to Randa and the **Europahütte** is signed right. Soon after there is another sign left to Randa. Our trail crosses the slope and the hut can be seen above. A few zigzags lead up to the original trail where there is a sign for the hut and also for the Domhütte path. This deviation probably adds on only about 100m of climbing but it feels hard at this stage of the walk, especially because the hut has been visible for some time.

After the hut there is an easy flat traverse which leads to a wobbly suspension bridge. (Presumably this is flexible so as to survive avalanche activity. It doesn't feel very stable.) The old path and bridge can be seen some way above.

Another spur is turned and there is a sign to Grächen (4hr30). Ahead the path is all too obvious – big sweeping zigzags leading upwards to cross a rocky slope eventually and pick up the traverse line again. From now on there are a lot of rocky sections and there are numerous sections where the path will clearly have to be remade almost on a yearly basis. It is really well waymarked but this must be a massive task.

A signed path descends to **Herbriggen**, after which the rocky section is relentless. There are not many safe places to stop. Any location for a rest or snack break should be chosen carefully. Look for grassy areas and check what is above before settling in.

The Matterhorn, which had disappeared from view just before the Europahütte, now reappears.

After much teetering from rock to rock (anyone who enjoys unstable boulder slopes will have a field day here) the path zigzags down and back up to a sign to Grächen (2hr40) and going the other way the Europahütte (2hr20) and Zermatt (8hr30).

After more rockiness a sign is reached pointing right to the Bordierhütte (2hr). A big grassy area can be seen, with a statue of St Bernard, the 11th century patron saint of alpinists, who established two hospices on high passes in the Alps to protect travellers and pilgrims. It is a pleasure for tired feet to reach this and enjoy the softness of grass rather than rocks. The view up the **Gasenried Gorge** is spectacular.

Go and pay your respects to St Bernard before heading down to pick up the path at a signpost: 1hr50 to Grächen, 2hr20 to St Niklaus; and, going the other way, 3hr30 to the Europahütte and 9hr40 to Zermatt.

So it's still quite a hike to the end and the descent is a killer for tired knees. However, if it hurts going down imagine going up!! And the whole thing is helped if the abundant alpenrose is in flower.

Some way down the descent into the woods there is a sign to the Bordierhütte on the right.

At a welcome flat track Grächen is signed right, but if you're going on down to St Niklaus you have to keep up the steep descent. The path is a bit vague at times but generally signed. It picks up a road near the bottom which is not very welcome, but finally comes out at a covered bridge over the river and into the village.

If you're looking for the bus, or are going to spend a night in **Grächen**, continue above Gasenried across the river and follow a waterway in the forest to reach the road at the top of Grächen village. Once in Grächen go down to the centre of the village to find the post office and the PTT bus stop. To walk down to **St Niklaus** from here go down the road out of the village and look out for signposts which cut the road and lead to back roads and down into the main valley.

VARIANT – ONE DAY

If you have just one day you can still do some of the Europaweg. You can either take the Sunnegga lift and walk as far as the descent to Randa, then take the train onwards to St Niklaus; or take the train down to Randa and walk up to meet the Europaweg just before the Europahütte, then continue along the Europaweg to Grächen. This is long and strenuous, but an excellent walk. For more details about the Europaweg check out www.europaweg.ch

ALTERNATIVE STAGE 1
Zermatt to St Niklaus valley route

Start	Zermatt
Access to start	Train from Visp; bus and road access to Täsch; train to Zermatt.
Altitude at start	1600m
Finish	St Niklaus
Access to finish	Train from Visp; train from Zermatt; bus from Visp; bus from Grächen; road access.
Altitude at finish	1120m
Altitude gain	0m
Altitude loss	500m
Distance	20km
Time	5hrs
Highpoint	Zermatt 1600m
Transport options	The train goes all the way!
Accommodation	Zermatt: lots of hotels; Täsch, Randa: hotels; St Niklaus: several hotels.
Extras	Take time to look around the villages passed en route as there are numerous old chalets and barns, and in the summer the flower-filled window boxes will be stunning.
Escape route	Bus down to Sion; train to Visp and Zermatt.

The route from Zermatt to St Niklaus by the valley foot-paths and back roads is by no means inferior to the higher route of the Europaweg, and there are several reasons why this route could be chosen instead. It may be that you need to reach St Niklaus in one day, in which case this is the route to take. If tired this walk is far kinder on legs and lungs than the undulating, fairly strenuous Europaweg; if the weather forecast is not good then this way is safer; this may be the first day of the trek, and thus a day to find those

Alpine legs. You may be well into the tour and 'viewed out' with high peaks, ready for a day spent enjoying the woods below Zermatt and then the villages all the way down the valley to St Niklaus. Whatever the reason for choosing this alternative, there are plenty of attractions to please both mind and body.

First is the delightful walk down to Täsch from Zermatt, often missed by those who think it's only from Zermatt that walks are worthwhile. Next visited is Randa, scene of several landslides in April and May 1991. The largest slip deposited 15 million cubic metres of rock and destroyed part of the little hamlet of Unterläch, as well as taking out the railway and road and blocking the Vierge river, which quickly began to flood the upper valley. The mass of debris remains an impressive sight.

Continuing down the valley, Herbriggen provides yet more traditional architecture before the final stroll past farms and vegetable gardens into St Niklaus, recognisable from afar for its fine onion-shaped church spire.

ROUTE

The whole route is the first half of the Zermatt marathon, which starts in St Niklaus and is discreetly signed with little marathon logos from time to time.

Begin with a lovely amble out down the main street of Zermatt and through the north end of town, scene of much recent construction work. The trail is reached from the far side of the railway station, up a flight of steps just by the tracks. This goes past the helicopter base and down past an old shack before crossing a churned-up section of hillside and across to grassy slopes. Take a last look back at the Matterhorn just as you round a grassy shoulder by a red bench – you won't see it again for a while. Now just follow the trail, often close to the railway, usually in the forest. There is a short section with a railing, and soon you'll emerge onto a wide track at the outskirts of Täsch. This leads past the campsite to the train station.

From here go across the lines to take a broad track which parallels the main road, staying on the other side of the river all the way down to Randa. Here the trail

Marmot and flowers

crosses over the river and skirts around the landslide then continues in the same fashion on one side of the river or the other, past Breitmatten and Herbriggen. At Mattsand a back road leads past several hamlets to St Niklaus.

TRANSHUMANCE

Transhumance describes the tradition whereby farmers move their cattle around according to seasonal changes, in search of optimum grazing conditions. In the Alps the farmer traditionally lives in a valley village in winter and keeps his cattle indoors in a barn. He does very little farming during the harsh cold months, just providing hay every day for his animals (a Swiss law decrees that cattle must be put outside at some stage every day throughout the year). As spring arrives the cattle are put out to graze the fresh grass in the lower meadows next to the village. As the weather warms up gradually the grass grows at higher altitudes. The farmer's first move will be to higher meadows not too far above the village. He will own a small farm there where he stays for several weeks whilst his animals graze these pastures; he milks them, and will often make cheese. This first stop-

off point is called a *mayen* in French, a word frequently encountered in place names whilst trekking in the Alps.

Once the summer is well established the farmer will take his cattle up to a higher farm (*alpage* in French) above the treeline, often around the 2000m mark. Here they will spend the rest of the summer, and the farmer will take his family to live up there too. Cheese will be produced for the winter, as well as other dairy products. They may also grow crops in the surrounding meadows, and in the past would certainly have grown enough for their own summer needs.

When the days begin to get shorter and colder it's time to head down to the village again. This is often a celebration in the Alps; a successful summer season means there will be enough food to keep everyone satisfied over the coming winter. The cattle may be adorned with flowers, and the whole village comes out to see their return. A few weeks are spent grazing the valley fields before once again the animals are quartered inside.

Transhumance is still practised throughout the Alps. When walking you will often come across *alpages*, and sometimes find cheese and milk for sale. Some of these summer farms also provide basic hut accommodation, and are often great places to stay where the evening meal will be a truly traditional affair.

Summer farm at Findeln above Zermatt

STAGE 2
St Niklaus to Gruben-Meiden

Start	St Niklaus
Access to start	Train from Visp; train from Zermatt; bus from Visp; bus from Grächen; road access.
Altitude at start	1120m
Finish	Gruben-Meiden
Access to finish	Summer bus from Sierre, road access.
Altitude of finish	1822m
Altitude gain	1790m; 896m if the cable car is used.
Altitude loss	1075m
Distance	12km
Time	8hrs without cable car; 5hrs with cable car.
Highpoint	Augstbordpass 2894m
Maps	1:50,000 Carte Nationale de la Suisse 5006 Matterhorn Mischabel; 1:25,000 Carte Nationale de la Suisse 1308 St Niklaus
Facilities	Gruben-Meiden is very small, but there is a tiny shop next to the Hotel Schwarzhorn. The hotel sells snack foods and chocolate.
Transport options	Jungu cable car.
Accommodation	St Niklaus: various hotels; Jungu: dormitory at restaurant; Gruben-Meiden: Hotel Schwarzhorn.
Extras	Above Jungu the trail becomes quite exposed for a short distance. Care should be taken here, especially in wet conditions. Névé often remains on the east slopes of the Augstbordpass, and the final section is quite steep; don't plan your trek for too early in the season, as the slopes could still be frozen.
Escape route	From the path junction before the final climb up to the Augstbordpass there is a path which heads down the Augstbordstafel to reach the Mattertal via Embd and Kalpetran. The train can be taken back to Zermatt.

St Niklaus is an attractive village. It's not a major centre, but for those undertaking the Tour of the Matterhorn it is situated in a convenient position in the Mattertal. Despite its small size, it has all the necessary facilities: bars, shops, restaurants, a few hotels and a post office.

In the 19th century the Mattertal rivalled any Alpine valley and St Niklaus was a much-visited town, rather like Chamonix in status. For a long time the parish of St Niklaus extended as far as the Theodulpass, and it was the economic capital of the Mattertal. Until as late as 1960 its population exceeded that of Zermatt. It was only in the early seventies that the motor road was extended from St Niklaus to Täsch – prior to that travel onwards up the valley had to be on foot, by mule or by train. Today the village is well served by bus and train, and being Swiss these services are reliable. However, you cannot see the Matterhorn from here.

For centuries the villages of the Mattertal exported goods such as cereals, salt and spices, as well as cattle and dairy products, over the Theodulpass. As a result the locals were experienced mountaineers, and St Niklaus was home to many Guides and alpinists. The

If you trek in the Alps in July the hillsides will be carpeted in pink alpenrose

Who could resist the restaurant at Jungu?

local names Knubel, Lochmatter and Imboden feature in many of the records of first ascents of major peaks of the region.

From St Niklaus the trek ascends to Jungu (1998m), a small hamlet perched in the most amazing position, generally accessed by a cable car that runs year-round. Time stands still here: just a few wooden chalets, a restaurant and a gleaming white church, all overlooking the Mattertal from a supremely sunny stance. In the summer the locals – even young girls dresssed in the latest gear, working like pros! – are to be seen scything the grass. Allow time to look around Jungu and savour the calm before heading on up into the hills. If you can spend the night here then do so – an evening spent on the terrace of the restaurant lapping up the views will be remembered forever.

The walk over the Augstbordpass is varied and exciting – from the grassy meadows of the village past one of the best viewpoints in the area, then on up to the rocky barren terrain that forms the pass. This route has been used for passage at least since Roman times, and traces of an old Roman road have been found. The pass carried the route from the Aosta Valley to the Rhône Valley, via the Theodulpass.

The other side of the col is no less beautiful – after some bouldery terrain the slopes become pastoral, and the final descent to Gruben-Meiden runs through larch forest. The village of Gruben-Meiden will not disappoint lovers of tranquil, unspoilt Alpine valleys. The valley is only occupied during the summer months and thus remains one of the wildest in the Alps. It stretches from the Rhône Valley to the foot of the Bishorn (4153m). In winter the road is closed at Oberems because there is often a risk of avalanche from the steep slopes further up the valley. Designated a Federal Reserve for Flora and Fauna, the Turtmanntal is a haven for lynx and chamois. Of course if you arrive on a Sunday in high season there will be lots of people and cars around, but away from the road and you'll soon find yourself in a bygone age, surrounded by grassy meadows, cows and burbling streams.

Heading around the Troara ridge

The Hotel Schwartzhorn is the only place to stay unless you're camping. You can either choose a room or a place in one of several dormitories – conveniently situated right at the top of the huge building – a four-flight climb nicely rounds off a full day in the hills!

ROUTE

From St Niklaus it is recommended that you take the cable car up to Jungu, not only to conserve energy for later in the day but also for the thrill of the ride – which is considerable.

If you are only going as far as Jungu today it is perhaps more sensible to walk than take the cable car. The trail is remarkably gentle when you consider the angle of the slope. From the cable car it appears a horrendous climb, but it's pleasant so long as you have the time to enjoy it.

The path starts innocuously enough from the base of the cable car, through meadows and into the forest, past a *bisse* (an irrigation waterway). Leaving the *bisse* the path climbs, and then crosses a rocky cleft by a footbridge. Again the path steepens; soon a series of white stations of the cross are found along the trail, dedicated by various families from the Mattertal. The presence of these suggests that praying for strength to climb the trail is called for, but very welcome red benches are to be found at strategic positions along the way (just in case the praying isn't enough!). There are several branches off the route, but all are signposted and you can't go

Stage 2: St Niklaus – Gruben Meiden

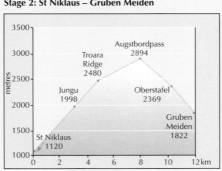

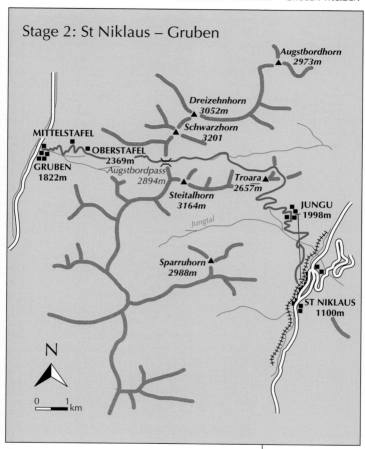

Stage 2: St Niklaus – Gruben

wrong. Zigzags eventually lead to the restaurant at **Jungu**, reached after about 3hrs.

Go through the village to the lift and then straight ahead into a park-like area where there is a lake; on especially hot and sunny days people may swim here. Beyond the lake exit onto the trail which has paint marks and goes west and up into the forest. It soon becomes well surfaced, wending up and back north. The flowery slopes are a delight, and after 45mins or so a well-placed bench at a signpost provides a good spot for a break. The trail leads up and out of the trees, now constructed from huge rock slabs. This relatively flat section of the route should be enjoyed to the full – take the time to look around as the views open up. It is not unusual to see herds of ibex grazing here. Ahead a huge cairn will be spotted in the distance, and this is *the* place from which to take in the view of the Mattertal peaks: the Nadelhorn, Lenspitze, Dom, Täschhorn, Breithorn and Weisshorn take pride of place. Definitely a place to linger a while.

From here, those who do not totally appreciate the delights of having space beneath their feet will have to take a deep breath – the path narrows to go up and around the rocky **Troara ridge** that leads into the Inner Tälli cwm below the Augstbordpass. The exposure is short-lived, and as long as there's no snow should not induce too many heart flutters. Once the shoulder is turned the ground flattens out and a rough track leads gently down through boulders and across several streams – some of them heard rather than seen. Rockfalls and avalanches from time to time destroy part of this trail, so be careful on any loose boulders. There is often snow remaining on these slopes, but it is usually easy to negotiate. Check out the unusual stacked roofs of the terraced houses at Augstbordstafel below.

After the streams the path climbs to a signpost, then continues though a sort of small gorge before attacking the final slopes to the **Augstbordpass**, which is all too evident up above. If there is névé here then hope that it's not still frozen – it shouldn't be unless the day is cloudy and the temperature very low. Take care if it is snowy, however, as the angle is steep enough for a slip to have serious consequences. In normal summer conditions you will be on slightly muddy scree and rock, and the ascent is nothing more than the usual Alpine grind.

The views from the top are fantastic: to the east you can even see as far as the Saastal peaks – notably the

Sunset from Gruben Meiden

Fletschorn and the Lagginhorn – whereas ahead lies the Turtmanntal and, beyond, the Meidzänd ridge.

The descent starts with a narrow path worn into the muddy grit – look out here for the rare king of the Alps, which flowers briefly around mid July. The path descends, then traverses left across a short section of bouldery scree before reaching a lake, just beyond and above which is a nice flat grassy area. Coming from the other direction this would be a good resting point before the final push to the col, but probably comes too soon for a stop on the way down. Zigzags give way to flatter meadows and a wonderful gentle amble down the Grüobtälli. The grassy slopes and tinkling streams are a welcome change from the austere scenery up on the col, and chamois frequently graze in this area.

After the farm at **Oberstafel** the slopes become more vegetated, with bilberry bushes, alpenrose and juniper forming a colourful carpet. It's not long before you find yourself once more in larch and spruce forest, where jays

99

and woodpeckers abound. A good trail makes for easy walking and before you know it you'll pop out right by the Hotel Schwarzhorn – very conveniently you arrive in the beer garden!

Do take a stroll round **Gruben-Meiden** – it only takes a few minutes and is delightful. On one memorable visit I arrived to find the church decked out in wild flowers for a local wedding and the resulting festivities involved everyone in the village, including hikers passing through. ◄

Note Although the hotel seems big and modern they do not like to take credit cards, so bring enough cash for your stay.

VARIANT
The Topalihütte, reached from Randa or by the new lift from St Niklaus, provides a good route to the Turtmanntal, going over the Wasulicke Pass and around the Jungtal to join the footpath up to the Augstbordpass.

Carline thistles are seen in meadows throughout the summer months

MARMOTS

Marmots could be described as the quintessential Alpine animal. They are about the size of a fat cat, with a big body and short legs. They have poor hearing and sight, but their sense of smell is acute.

Marmots spend the summer months eating as much as they can so as to be as fat as possible by the time they head to the burrow for the winter hibernation, which lasts from 6 to 8 months. A full-size adult will

be around 5 kilos in October, but when it emerges in late April or May will weigh only about 2 kilos. In this weakened state the marmot is an easy target for birds of prey or foxes.

Marmots wake up from hibernation by instinct, regardless of temperature or conditions. They leave the winter burrow and ascend to a higher summer burrow, which is generally situated on sun-

Marmots have poor sight and hearing, so if you're downwind you have a chance of a good view

nier slopes. May is the season of romance, and 35 days later the babies are born.

Their colour varies from very light fawn to brown to almost black, and they live on grassy or bouldery slopes from 1300m up to about 2500–3000m. On their summer 'all you can eat' programme marmots need to consume 400g of greens at every meal. They add a bit of variety with insects such as larvae or grasshoppers.

An afternoon siesta helps with digestion before the evening gastronomic extravaganza, and marmots can often be seen soaking up the rays on flat rocks during this part of the day. With a bit of luck they can live for 14–16 years.

STAGE 3
Gruben-Meiden to Zinal

Start	Gruben-Meiden
Access to start	Bus and cable car from Sierre; road access.
Altitude at start	1822m
Finish	Zinal
Access to finish	Bus from Sierre; road access.
Altitude at finish	1660m
Altitude gain	965m
Altitude loss	1140m
Distance	19km
Time	8hrs (5hrs to the Hotel Weisshorn; 3hrs on to Zinal).
Highpoint	Meidpass 2790m
Maps	1:50,000 Carte Nationale de la Suisse 5006 Matterhorn Mischabel; 1:25,000 Carte Nationale de la Suisse 1308 St Niklaus, 1307 Vissoie, 1327 Evolène
Facilities	Hotel Weisshorn is a good place to stop, and sells drinks and lunch foods. Zinal has all necessary facilities, including a good bakery.
Transport options	None
Accommodation	Gruben-Meiden: Hotel Schwarzhorn; Hotel Weisshorn; Zinal: several hotels, gîte Auberge Alpina.
Extras	The long high-level traversing path from the Hotel Weisshorn to Zinal is the route of one of the Alps' most famous and scenic running races: the Sierre Zinal race, which starts down in the Rhône Valley at Sierre and climbs up to the Hotel Weisshorn then onwards to Zinal. This takes place on the second Sunday of August so it's probably best to avoid this stage on that day – or be prepared to move over frequently as the runners will be coming from behind you! There is a walker's category for those interested.
Escape route	There are really no options on the ascent from the Turt-manntal, but from the Hotel Weisshorn and from several

places along the trail to Zinal paths descend to the Val d'Anniviers. From there buses connect with the train in the Rhône Valley to go back up the Mattertal. Buses also run up the Val d'Anniviers to Zinal.

This is one of the most delightful stages of the trek as it provides wonderful and varied mountain views – you get to see at least four and, with a bit of luck, five summits which surpass the magic 4000m figure; the terrain is wild and unspoilt; and you're heading for Zinal, one of the nicest Alpine towns around. Here is a resort where restraint has been exercised: there are cable cars and hotels and plenty of other tourist attractions, but they do not smother the authentic feel of the village, which remains a pleasure to visit. The name Zinal apparently comes from the patois word *tséna*, denoting the shape of the valley, which is like a water channel. In the old days Zinal was just a summer village used for transhumance. Today it's a bustling year-round centre for permanent residents and visitors alike.

The Hotel Weisshorn enjoys brilliant views

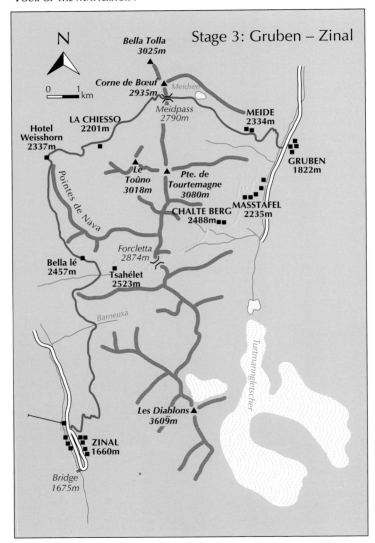

N

0   1
km

Stage 3: Gruben – Zinal

Bella Tolla
3025m

Corne de Bœuf
2935m

Meidsee

Meidpass
2790m

LA CHIESSO
2201m

MEIDE
2334m

Hotel
Weisshorn
2337m

GRUBEN
1822m

Le
Toûno
3018m

Pte. de
Tourtemagne
3080m

Pointes de Nava

MASSTAFEL
2235m

CHALTE BERG
2488m

Forcletta
2874m

Bella lé
2457m

Tsahélet
2523m

Barneuxa

Turtmanngletscher

Les Diablons
3609m

ZINAL
1660m

Bridge
1675m

The big question on this stage is whether to go over the Meidpass and stay at the Hotel Weisshorn, or whether to take the shorter version of the route via Forcletta (see alternative Stage 3) and thus get to Zinal in the day. The Hotel Weisshorn (2337m) offers a unique experience, as it is built in true Victorian style, perched grandly above the Val d'Anniviers, at the upper limit of the alpages. It was opened to cater for English visitors in 1882, offering 'bath, heating, electricity, telephone, horses, mules and carriages'. It has been restored fairly recently but retains its old charm and slight air of eccentricity. If you stay here you have a fairly restful walk the following day to Zinal. Whilst it is perfectly feasible to go from the Hotel Weisshorn on over to Moiry (see Stage 4) in the day, it would be a shame to miss out on exploring Zinal's back

Stage 3: Gruben Meiden – Zinal

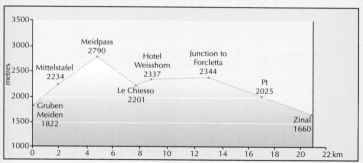

streets and old wooden chalets, not to mention the pâtisserie and tempting cafés. If possible, enjoy a pleasant day over to the Hotel Weisshorn then a nice half-day amble along the high-level traversing path to Zinal, with time to rest and resupply once there. The Forcletta option is good for those with fewer days to spare and is equally beautiful and, if anything, a little more remote and wild than the Meidpass.

Whichever route is taken you will move from German- to French-speaking Switzerland when you cross the Meidpass, the highpoint of the day. Also – whichever route is taken – the final part of the walk takes the same balcony trail which meanders high above the Val d'Anniviers. If the weather is favourable, five 4000m peaks can be seen from this high traverse: the Weisshorn, Zinal Rothorn, Obergabelhorn, Dent Blanche and (if it's really clear, and only for a short time) the Matterhorn – it's the pointy one at the back. This is a really great part of the walk and one to savour to the full.

ROUTE

Today's stage offers a choice of routes to Zinal: either via the Meidpass, with an option of overnighting at Hotel Weisshorn, or to Zinal in one day via the Forcletta Pass.

From the Hotel Schwarzhorn head across the river and up into the forest. Initially steep, the angle eases as the path takes a long zigzag though the dense woods, eventually emerging near the farms of Mittel and Ober Stafel (**Meide**). Now the way is easy and obvious, up the gentle Meidtälli cwm past a lovely small lake at Chleis Seeroji (2520m) where the high peaks are reflected in the water, making for excellent photographs. A bigger lake, the Meidsee, is soon passed above, after which it's a short distance to the **Meidpass**.

Looking back, the Augstbordpass route is very clear. Next to the Meidpass is the Meidspitz, and the ridge leading to the Bella Tolla (3025m). This can be ascended in good weather and makes a great extra to the day (see variant). Views to the south are dominated by the Bishorn and the north ridge of the Weisshorn; with binoculars you'll be able to see the track up the Normal Route of the Bishorn, a very popular 4000m peak.

The descent from the Meidpass leads into the somewhat featureless Montagne de Roua, a gently angled basin surrounded by rocky peaks, one of which is Le Toûno (to the south).

Down below the white edifice of the Hotel Weisshorn stands proud, and in good visibility it's easy to see the way. In foggy conditions you need to keep a good eye on the route as you could stray off course and find yourself heading down to St Luc if you're not careful.

Once past the buildings at **Le Chiesso** (2201m), there is a brief climb to reach **Hotel Weisshorn**. From here there are wide-ranging views right across to the far side of the Rhône Valley, and the long sloping summit of Les Diablerets can clearly be seen. If you spend the night here it's wonderful to be so high up above the twinkling lights of the villages far below. It's easy to see why 19th-century travellers were enamoured with the place.

From the hotel the trail is marked to Zinal, and frequent yellow Zs on rocks also mark the route of the famous fell race. The walk begins with a very short ascent, then it's pretty flat for several kilometres. For much of the way the terrain is kind underfoot, so you can enjoy the views without the risk of falling off the path. Far below is the Val d'Anniviers with the towns and villages of Vissoie, St Luc, Grimentz and Ayer, amongst others. Allow plenty of time for this section because it really is fabulous: in the early summer the slopes are covered in flowers, ranging from anemones and gentians to alpenrose, orange hawksbeard and pinks to monkshood and,

The Bishorn and the Weisshorn seen from the route up to Forcletta (variant)

107

as autumn approaches, the red leaves of the bilberry. If you are on the trail early in the morning you are quite likely to spot chamois grazing.

Eventually you'll come across a very small building and the junction to the Forcletta. Just beyond is a wooden footbridge over a stream, a good place to stop for a break. The path continues pretty much the same, but with a section of boulders where in wet conditions you need to watch your footing – it would be all too easy to turn an ankle here. There is a rather grand entrance to the Bella Lé farm, celebrating the 25th anniversary of the Sierre Zinal race, and just beyond, away in the distance the Matterhorn timidly makes an appearance – if you're lucky!

The treeline is only just below now, but there's still a way to go before the path finally plunges into the shade of the larch forest and begins its descent to Zinal. The last part is steep and knee crunching, but bear with it: you'll soon be there. Emerging onto the road check out the numbers painted on the tarmac – from 500m they

A typical old wooden barn

108

drop down to 100m as you get to the edge of **Zinal**, this being the final countdown for the Sierre Zinal race.

Walk along the road, then down onto the main road by an area with a bench and a fountain, just opposite the cable car. Turn left into the centre, and the tourist office is found on the left. For the old part of town stay on the road you came in on; it parallels the main road. The Auberge Alpina, which offers dormitory accommodation, is at the far end of town.

VARIANT

From the Meidpass the Bella Tolla (3025m) is an optional summit and well worthwhile if you have time, energy and good weather. Bella Tolla is the highpoint of the ridge separating the Turtmannatal from the Valle d'Anniviers, and from its summit there is a 360-degree view from the Bernese and Valaisan Alps to the Mont Blanc massif. If you choose to go this way there is no need to return to the col as there is a path leading directly down from the top. At the Lac de la Bella Tolla you need to head left (south), past the Lac de l'Armina to pick up the regular trail near the unnamed lake pt.2544.

CHAMOIS

The chamois is a mountain goat, and can be seen throughout the Alps. It is not protected, except in National Parks or reserves, but there is a limited hunting season and hunters are subject to a strict quota. The chamois is not only valued for its horns but also for its meat and skin.

Both male and female chamois have relatively small horns that hook back. The animals are beige/brown in summer, but the coat darkens considerably for the winter months.

The female chamois give birth to one or two young in June, weighing about 2 kilos, after 180 days of gestation. Four days after their birth the young can run as fast as the herd, and after one week the mother rejoins her herd, which is led by a sterile female. Four months of suckling follow until the rutting season in mid November, at which time the young are sent to join the herd of young chamois until they reach sexual maturity at 18 months.

It's rare to be able to get close to chamois

If the chamois survive their first winter they can live up to 15–25 years, and the males can reach a weight of 25 kilos. They are lovers of cold, and in summer will often be seen hanging out on shady slopes of névé. They are particularly adept on steep terrain and can be spotted from afar racing across tortuous hillsides, but they also spend much of the year in the forests. Chamois are timid creatures, unlikely to let you get close.

ALTERNATIVE STAGE 3

Gruben-Meiden to Zinal via the Forcletta

Start	Gruben-Meiden
Access to start	Bus and cable car from Sierre; road access.
Altitude at start	1822m
Finish	Zinal
Access to finish	Bus from Sierre; road access.
Altitude at finish	1660m
Altitude gain	1052m
Altitude loss	1214m
Distance	14.5km
Time	6–7hrs
Highpoint	Forcletta 2874m
Transport options	None
Accommodation	Gruben-Meiden: Hotel Schwartzhorn; Zinal: several hotels; *gîte* Auberge Alpina.
Escape route	There are no options on this route other than to retrace your steps.

ROUTE

Take the road south out of the village up the valley for about 1km to a large wooden bridge over the river. The footpath heads up into the forest from here and rises in a series of somewhat overgrown zigzags to finally emerge into higher meadows. A track is soon reached which you follow up to the farm buildings at **Chalte Berg** (2488m). There has been a lot of recent building here – the footpath may have been redirected – but just take the easiest option to soon pick up a good waymarked trail that goes southwest around the hillside into a beautiful wild area of small lakes and rocky slopes.

The Forcletta Pass (2874m) provides a short cut over to Zinal, avoiding the Hotel Weisshorn. This way presents no extra difficulties.

The way is now steady up the Blüomattälli cwm to the somewhat barren **Forcletta Pass**. You will enjoy fine views of the Brunneghorn and the Bishorn as you make this final ascent.

From the col the descent route is easy to follow in long zigzags down shale and scree, through some boulders to a pleasant grassy area just above the **Tsahélet farm** at 2523m. A flat rock next to a cross beckons for a last picnic stop before heading on down.

Keep your eye on the path for the next part as it descends wet and marshy slopes to a small wooden building on the main trail from the Hotel Weisshorn. Turn left and follow this trail as in the main description all the way to **Zinal**.

The route from the Hotel Weisshorn to Zinal enjoys some of the best views around

STAGE 4
Zinal to Les Haudères and Arolla

Start	Zinal
Access to start	Bus from Sierre; road access.
Altitude at start	1660m
Finish	Les Haudères
Access to finish	Bus from Sion; road access.
Altitude at finish	1450m
Altitude gain	1975m: 1185m Zinal to Col de Sorebois; 790m Moiry Lake to Les Haudères.
Altitude loss	2180m: 710m Col de Sorebois to Moiry Lake; 1470m Col de Torrent to Les Haudères.
Distance	22km (9.5km Zinal to Moiry Lake)
Time	11hrs
Highpoint	Col de Torrent 2919m
Maps	1:50,000 Carte Nationale de la Suisse 5006 Matterhorn Mischabel; 1:25,000 Carte Nationale de la Suisse 1307 Vissoie, 1327 Evolène
Facilities	Moiry restaurant has some snacks for sale and their food is excellent. Arolla has a supermarket and a very good little store, as well as an excellent sports shop.
Transport options	Cable car from Zinal; bus service from Villa to Les Haudères.
Accommodation	Zinal: several hotels; gîte Auberge Alpina; Moiry Lake restaurant dormitory; Les Haudères: several hotels.
Extras	Moiry Lake can be accessed by bus from Grimentz and also by road. By taking the lift out of Zinal and the bus from Villa to Les Haudères this stage could be completed in one long day. However, a stay at the Moiry Lake is very pleasant, and you can then do the Tour du Lac as an afternoon excursion – or sit at the café and sample the Swiss fare.
Escape route	From Moiry there is a summer bus service to Grimentz, from where the bus can be picked up down to the Rhône Valley. Train back to Zermatt.

This fourth stage from Zinal to Les Haudères gives gentle and pastoral walking, a welcome change from the rocky terrain encountered on most high passes. However, all around are high, glaciated peaks with soaring rocky ridges, attesting to the fact that this is very much the heart of the Alps. These spectacular views can be enjoyed to the full as the terrain underfoot does not require too much concentration.

Access to Stage 5
Most people take the bus from Les Haudères to Arolla (the start of Stage 5 – but see details for the walking link route on p121). This could be done in the evening at the end of Stage 4, thereby staying in Arolla rather than Les Haudères. Arolla is a very small village but enjoys a renown totally out of proportion to its size. It is a popular base for Alpinists aspiring to the many accessible glaciated peaks in the area. Arolla has only had road access since 1960 and its old name was *l'enfer blanc* – the white hell.

On the ascent out of Zinal the views are dominated by the huge peaks of the Weisshorn and the Zinal Rothorn. Once at the Col de Sorebois new summits are to be seen, along with the tumbling chaotic Moiry Glacier, whilst the Col de Torrent reserves yet more surprises: from there the view extends – on a good day – all the way to Mont Blanc. Even if Mont Blanc is not visible the chances are you'll get your first views of other big summits such as the Grand Combin, Pigne d'Arolla and Mont Blanc de Cheilon. On the descent the North Face of the Pigne d'Arolla is seen in all its splendour.

The Val d'Hérens, the end of this stage, leads right up to the base of the Dent Blanche, and Les Haudères is in the shadow of this huge, imposing summit. Further down the valley the small town of Evolène is one of the most traditional in Switzerland. Interestingly its local dialect is almost identical to those of the Italian valleys of Valpelline and Valtournanche, compelling proof of the trade that has gone on for centuries between these Alpine valleys.

The black Hérens cows are named after this valley, and will be seen on many occasions during this stage. In addition to wildlife the sunny slopes above Villa are a haven for flora, and throughout the summer you will be bombarded by colours and scents. Once in Les Haudères it's worth taking time to explore the side streets and amazingly old chalets. This is the last old village for an overnight stay until the return to Zermatt.

ROUTE

The path takes the meadows up from the car park at the end of the village. Zigzags wend up through forest and then emerge at a farm building. Continue up again before trending across right (north) to the top of the cable car at **Sorebois**. There is a very good self-service café here with a panoramic terrace – the views of the Weisshorn and the Zinal Rothorn are particularly splendid.

There are two options to reach the Col de Sorebois (2835m): path or cable car. If you're staying at Auberge Alpina the path is right opposite, ideal if you're not short of time or energy.

Reaching the Col de Sorebois above Moiry Lake

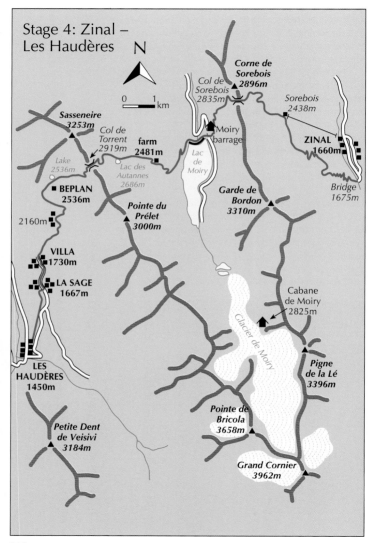

Stage 4: Zinal – Les Haudères

N

0   1 km

Sasseneire
3253m

Col de Torrent
2919m

farm
2481m

Col de Sorebois
2835m

Corne de Sorebois
2896m

Sorebois
2438m

Moiry barrage

ZINAL
1660m

Lac de Moiry

Bridge
1675m

Lake
2536m

Lac des Autannes
2686m

BEPLAN
2536m

Pointe du Prélet
3000m

Garde de Bordon
3310m

2160m

VILLA
1730m

LA SAGE
1667m

Cabane de Moiry
2825m

Glacier de Moiry

Pigne de la Lé
3396m

LES HAUDÈRES
1450m

Petite Dent de Veisivi
3184m

Pointe de Bricola
3658m

Grand Cornier
3962m

(A longer route to Sorebois from Zinal is to go via the Petit Mountet hut. Take the well-travelled track south out of Zinal, following the river, then at a sign turn right. The path from the hut to the lift then takes a long, gently rising traverse.)

From the lift to the Col de Sorebois it's best to fall into conversation with a fellow hiker or disappear into your own thoughts for an hour or so as this is not the prettiest terrain. Follow muddy and gravelly bulldozed ski pistes in a generally northwest then westerly direction. Most pistes lead to the same place so you can't get lost unless it's foggy, in which case you'll need to be careful and maybe even take a bearing.

Once at the **Col de Sorebois** you can open your eyes again – ahead lies the incredibly turquoise-blue **Moiry Lake**, and behind are the Zinal summits. Everything looks a lot better from up here. The slopes on the far side of Sorebois are home to chamois, and if you're lucky you may well spot a herd grazing, or fleeing away from you across the mountain.

The path down is really well graded and leads in zig-zags to a flattening on a spur. Head down grassy slopes, often grazed by sturdy black Hérens cows, to a dark

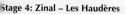

Stage 4: Zinal – Les Haudères

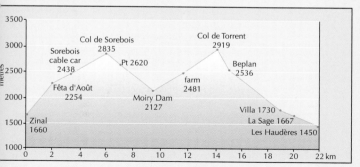

117

The Moiry peaks seen on the ascent to the Col de Torrent

wooden building on the right. This is the dormitory, part of the Moiry restaurant complex. If you're staying here leave your sacs and go down to the restaurant to get the key. Since you eat at the restaurant you'll get an extra workout by ascending the 100m between the two buildings several times during the evening. This slope is home to many marmots, and the early evening tends to see a lot of activity especially when the youngsters are around.

From the middle of the dam there is a fine view up towards the Moiry Glacier and beyond to the Grand Cornier. Go over the dam and up the obvious track that winds south around the hillside, then west and up to a summer dairy farm. Here the track becomes a typical footpath heading up through pastures. The views of the glacier and peaks open up, and once you reach the **Lac des Autannes** they really are superb. The Moiry hut can just be discerned, perched on a rocky promontory high above the glacier.

The path is flat before climbing again, this time more steeply, to approach the **Col de Torrent** (2919m) from the right (north). And what a viewpoint this is. If you're lucky and it's really clear you can see Mont Blanc a very long way to the west. Nearer are the Arolla peaks, the Pigne d'Arolla and Mont Blanc de Cheilon.

The col has a fine cross and is definitely one of the highpoints of this stage. It's a popular day walk from Moiry, as well as being on the Chamonix Zermatt Walkers' Route, so don't expect to be alone. However, if you are tempted to go higher then either go left or right and you can attain little sub-summits that give even better views and some exposure.

Below the Val d'Hérens can be seen, the slopes scattered with picture-postcard chalets. After the usual barren rocky start the terrain soon becomes grassy, and in little time a pond near **Beplan** is reached. This can be a delight if you are there before the cows have been brought up, and is a great place for a stop. However, the cows can make it pretty muddy round the edges and it's preferable to continue on a little along a rounded shoulder, adorned with pinky orange limestone outcrops. If you're lucky you might find edelweiss hiding out here.

This hillside is a lovely vantage point so don't rush it; you'll be down in the valley soon enough. There are dozens of spots crying out for you to stop and take a break – why not have a lazy time of it, and amble down slowly.

Reaching a track, you'll find the trail signposted to the right, and then down past several chalets. The route has already seen a few changes around here due to construction, but it will certainly be signposted as new owners don't really want you wandering through their gardens – just keep your eyes open.

Lower down the path crosses a stream and finally takes a paved track to pop out among the charming old chalets of **Villa**.

Either take the bus, or go down the road for a kilometre or so to the next village, **La Sage**. Here a nifty little alley slips off to the right and down onto a back road that then becomes a bush-bordered path, much favoured by locals for walking their dogs. This is actually a very pleasant way to reach **Les Haudères**, in an easy hour from Villa.

VARIANT

The Cabane de Moiry is situated high up on the eastern slopes of the Moiry Glacier, and is an optional extra for this stage. A visit there is recommended for the impressive views of the glacier, which splits into deep blue crevasses near its snout. The high peaks are also impressive, notably the Grand Cornier and the Pointes de Bricola and de Murti. However, it should be noted that the hut can be quite crowded thanks to its relative ease of access and the abundance of nearby Alpine peaks that sport moderate routes.

To reach the Moiry hut from the Sorebois there are three possibilities:

- Follow the road along the lake then head up the footpath, or

- Just above the Moiry restaurant dormitory, head off left (south) along an undulating path that contours around, staying high above the road to join the hut path. This trail is signed as the Tour du Lac (2500m) as it hugs that altitude for much of the way.

- Finally, from below the farm on the descent from the Col de Torrent the Tour du Lac is signed, and by following this you take the trail around the lake to the far end, then follow the path up to the hut.

From the Cabane de Moiry, or from the southern end of the Moiry Lake, there is an alternative way to reach Les Haudères by going over the Col du Tsaté (2868m) and then down to la Forclaz, which is just above Les Haudères.

LINK ROUTE
Les Haudères to Arolla

Start	Les Haudères
Access to start	Bus from Sion; road access.
Altitude at start	1450m
Finish	Arolla
Access to finish	Bus from Sion; road access.
Altitude at finish	2006m
Altitude gain	585m
Altitude loss	85m
Distance	8km
Time	3–3hrs 30mins
Highpoint	Pra Gra 2164m
Transport options	Bus from Les Haudères to Arolla.
Accommodation	Les Haudères: several hotels; Arolla: several hotels.
Extras	The first part, from Les Haudères to Lac Bleu, does not have much to recommend it. However, from Lac Bleu to Arolla is a pleasant and interesting walk.
Escape route	Train back to Zermatt.

Walking from Les Haudères to Arolla is not really an integral part of the Tour of the Matterhorn as it just links the two places, with little special in the way of sights and terrain. If you do decide to walk it, it needs to be a short day, as beyond Arolla there is no more accommodation before the Rifugio Collon-Nacamuli after the Col Collon, and you do not want to be toiling up the Haut Glacier d'Arolla in late afternoon heat.

This stage is generally missed out since the bus provides a convenient alternative. However, for those with plenty of time and wishing to walk, why not?

ROUTE

Take the main road out of **Les Haudères** until you find a signed track on the left, leading alongside the river. This takes a gentle route up past old wooden chalets

121

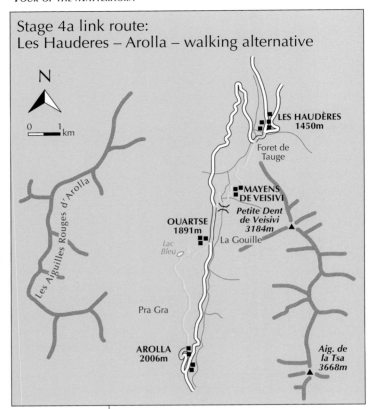

Stage 4a link route:
Les Hauderes – Arolla – walking alternative

surrounded by meadows. At all forks go straight ahead. Finally turn right over the river and follow a trail past a small oratory and then next to the road. It comes out onto the road near **La Gouille**. Turn left; after about 200m enter the small hamlet. The footpath continues upwards to the outflow of the aptly named **Lac Bleu**, and above this to a grassy bluff. From here there are good views not only of the lake but also of Mont Collon. Continue on the good trail, signed to Arolla, which crosses several streams then zigzags up to reach open hillsides. From here the Pigne d'Arolla comes into view, as well as the omnipresent Mont Collon. The hamlet of Pra Gra is passed as the path continues to climb. It then descends for some way, past several junctions, to reach woods just before arriving in **Arolla** by the Centre Alpin. From here it's a quick descent to the road into the village, past the Hotel du Glacier.

HÉRENS COWS

Whilst trekking in the Alps you are almost certain to see many different sorts of cows. They are all beautiful, and should not be feared. When you go past them try not to scare them with your trekking poles. Although in general it is wise to keep a safe distance from their rear ends, it's worth taking the time to say hello and, if they want to, let them lick your hand – they like to lick anything salty.

One particular type of cow will draw your attention. This is the dark brown or black Hérens cow, which is a race apart. This breed is very hardy and muscular and has a natural fighting tendency – not towards humans, but towards each other. The females will fight for dominance of the herd. They do not hurt each other – it's more a matter of intimidation – but the winner is the one who holds out the longest without backing off. This cow will then lead the herd for the season, and generally wears the biggest bell.

Big, black and very sturdy, the Hérens is an impressive breed of cow

The local farmers hold regular contests between their cows, *Combat des Reines*, where each farmer presents his bravest cow and they have a stand-off. Such events are worth going to if you happen to be around at the time, as they are seen as both a celebration of these fabulous animals and an excuse for a party.

STAGE 5
Arolla to Prarayer

Start	Arolla
Access to start	Bus from Sion; road access.
Altitude at start	2006m
Finish	Prarayer
Access to finish	Bus to Valpelline; taxi onwards to the end of the road. Road access as far as Place Moulin next to the dam at the south-west end of the lake, 3km from Prarayer.
Altitude at finish	2005m
Altitude gain	108m
Altitude loss	1085m
Distance	15km
Time	9hrs
Highpoint	Col Collon 3087m (or 3114m on the Italian map!)
Maps	1:50,000 Carte Nationale de la Suisse 5006 Matterhorn Mischabel; Istituto Geografico Centrale 5 Cervino-Matterhorn e Monte Rosa 1:25,000 Carte Nationale de la Suisse 1347 Matterhorn; Istituto Geografico Centrale 115 La Valpelline, Valle di Ollomont, Valle di St Barthélmeny
Facilities	There are no facilities after Arolla until you reach the Rifugio Collon-Nacamuli.
Transport options	None
Accommodation	Arolla: several hotels; Rifugio Collon-Nacamuli; Rifugio Prarayer. Cabane des Bouquelins (emergency hut).
Extras	The walk out of Arolla can be shortened if you have access to wheeled transport; cars can be parked 2km out of the village at the end of the track. The Italian map shows a glacier on the Italian side of the Col Collon, but this is long gone and scree and moraine slopes are all that remain.
Escape route	Once embarked on this stage there is really no escape route other than back to Arolla the way you've come. If a problem arose after passing the Col Collon you would need to think care-

fully about whether it would be easier to go down (then have the hassle of returning to Switzerland from Italy) or turn back and perhaps have a longer return route within Switzerland.

Depending where the trek is started, the ascent to Col Collon (3087m) is likely to be the first glacier crossing encountered. This is an exciting part of the tour as it takes you up into the high mountains, a world normally reserved for those who are climbing peaks. All around are snowy mountains and high rocky summits.

Whilst not difficult, the glacier should not be underestimated: in dry conditions a rope will probably not be needed for most of the way, but as soon as snow covers the ice it is advisable to rope up, as crevasses cannot be seen in fresh snow. Sometimes the whole climb can be accomplished without using crampons, by following the stony moraines until the flatter terrain near the col is reached. However, this can be rather tortuous, and just a couple of metres of sloping ice can result in a slip. This may leave you sliding a long way over ice and gravel which is not very pleasant. It is much quicker and generally more comfortable to put on crampons if there is ice to be crossed, rather than teetering from one rocky island to another.

The climb out from Arolla is long – a good 5hrs 30mins to 6 hrs to the col – but one with plenty of variety and enjoyment. On the other side, in Italy, the terrain changes from glacier to moraine and glacier-hewn rocks before plunging down into beautiful Alpine meadows where marmots and wild flowers abound.

The Col Collon has been a much-used pass for centuries. From around AD1220 a band of villains from Evolène regularly raided the Valpelline village of Bionaz, which resulted in reciprocal raiding from the Valpelline people. In 1233 a peace treaty was signed between the two valleys, which was reiterated 100 years later with a pact to provide mutual help between the towns. From

Reaching the Col Collon

thereon there has been an agreement that allows the Evolène farmers to graze their cattle over in the Valpelline Valley. Good relations continued, with much trade between the valleys, but the advance of the glaciers in the 18th century changed all this. Soon only alpinists could cross the col, and 64 sheep were killed in a storm there in 1859.

The Rifugio Collon-Nacamuli (2818m) would provide an excellent overnight to shorten this day, and if you are not pushed for time this can be recommended. Otherwise the next accommodation is down in the valley at the northeast end of the incredibly blue Place Moulin Lake. A flat track runs along the shore of the lake, and the Rifugio Prarayer offers typical Italian lunchtime fare, so it's a popular spot for families to walk the *bambinos*, grandparents and the dog. Weekends and holidays are especially bustling and festive, but in the evening calm descends on Prarayer again and the stunning surroundings can be enjoyed to the full. The Rifugio Prarayer provides excellent accommodation and food and a very warm welcome.

Before the dam was built Prarayer was a thriving village where cereals were cultivated and cattle farmed. In the warmer climes of the Middle Ages there was much traffic over the Col Collon, non-glaciated in those days. Smuggling continued over this col until the 1970s when frontiers started to open up.

At Prarayer there is a plaque commemorating a visit by Achille Rati, the future Pope Pius IX, who was a keen Alpinist. Wildlife abounds in this region, and you may well glimpse chamois grazing the higher slopes as you descend from the col. It is not rare to see or hear black grouse in the surrounding larch forests.

On the Haut Glacier d'Arolla – Mont Brulé dominates ahead

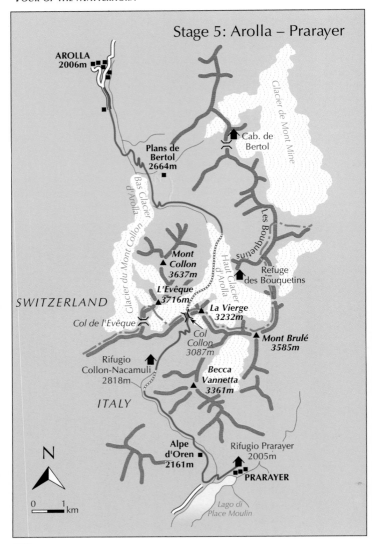

Stage 5: Arolla – Prarayer

AROLLA
2006m

Plans de
Bertol
2664m

Cab. de
Bertol

Glacier de Mont Mine

Bas Glacier d'Arolla

Les Bouquetins

Glacier du Mont Collon

Mont
Collon
3637m

Haut Glacier d'Arolla

Refuge
des Bouquetins

SWITZERLAND

L'Evêque
3716m

La Vierge
3232m

Col de l'Evêque

Col
Collon
3087m

Mont Brulé
3585m

Rifugio
Collon-Nacamuli
2818m

Becca
Vannetta
3361m

ITALY

N

Alpe
d'Oren
2161m

Rifugio Prarayer
2005m

PRARAYER

0   1 km

Lago di
Place Moulin

ROUTE

Leave Arolla by the road heading south, which soon becomes a dirt track. After a couple of kilometres the road ends, and a footpath continues heading up the left (east) side of the valley. Ahead are the steep slopes of the North Face of Mont Collon. This trail leads to the Cabane de Bertol as well as the Col Collon, and we follow this route for some way towards the Plans de Bertol. There is a choice: the old path stays low and skirts round under the rocky shoulder to the **Bas Glacier d'Arolla**, whilst the signed way goes up to the **Plans de Bertol** then leaves the hut path and descends to join this path going to the glacier. The lower path is now signed as out of use and the path makers want us to use the higher path. In summer 2008 the lower path was still feasible but I am not sure how long it will remain so. Whichever path is taken you will come to the moraine and boulderfields which give access to the Haut Glacier d'Arolla and there is a signpost (which rather optimistically gives 2hrs 45mins to the col), and red and white waymarks lead onwards.

Views open up with the Pigne d'Arolla to the southwest and the Bouquetins to the east. As the path nears

The trek for the next two days (stages 5 and 6) is quite committing, and should not be undertaken lightly – bad weather or a lack of trek preparation would be reasons to change your plans.

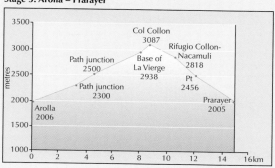

Stage 5: Arolla – Prarayer

129

On the moraine slopes under the Rifugio Collon-Nacamuli

the glacier the waymarks change to blue and white to lead up a moraine ridge. In some places there are blue and white posts to show the way, but these tend to get disturbed by the movement of the ice underneath so it's best to try to plan a route up the glacier by sight rather than blindly going from pole to pole.

Once on the glacier just follow your nose, taking the easiest line. To begin with it will be easier to follow the medial moraines which provide grippy rocks, but probably as you gain height these rocky section will become intermittent and it will be quicker to put on crampons and stick to the ice. If there is fresh snow then do rope up.

The prominent rocky bastion of the Vierge divides the glacier, and we head up a steeper slope to its right. (In the last couple of years this slope has lost its ice and is mainly moraine rubble. If you're wearing crampons you may have to take them off for this section.) The angles eases as the **Col Collon** is reached, and once there it's time to absorb those views. Just next to the col the snowy west slopes of Mont Brulé often have tracks on them; much further away is the Dent d'Hérens.

Be sure to find the way as you leave the col. Don't set off directly down; the trail strikes across left and slightly up to a signpost which gives 45mins to the **Rifugio Collon-Nacamuli**. From this point the way weaves down and back right, marked by yellow waymarks. This first part of the trail could be difficult to find in fog or névé, but further down the way is clearer and leads

Rifugio Collon-Nacamuli

The Place Moulin Lake with its incredibly blue water

around towards the hut. When the path goes right and up to the hut there is a vague traverse across which avoids actually going to the hut. Take this if you see it, or go on up to the hut, then descend and meet the traverse further down at a signpost.

The signs of glacial activity are all too evident here – glacially polished rocks and moraines attest to the fact that not long ago this side of the col also had its glacier. A couple of glacial lakes are passed before the trail tackles steep ground by means of tight zigzags and some metal rung footholds. Finally this slope ends at a flat area dominated by a huge moraine. Here the scenery is wild and remote, and after the rigours of the descent this is surely a place to rest and savour.

The difficulties are now over, and from here on you can relax and amble along the delightful Comba d'Oren where marmots will scurry for their burrows as you pass. Wild flowers are everywhere as the trail winds in and out of boulders, across streams, then follows an irrigation *bisse* to an Alpine farm at **Oren** (2161m).

A path must break off from here to descend directly to Prarayer, but it is not obvious and maybe the farmer is not keen on people crossing his land. If you miss it then continue (as I have done each time) on the main trail, which is extremely pleasant and gives great views of the bright blue waters of Lago di Place Moulin below. The Comba di Valcournera can be seen on the other side of the valley, the next stage of the trek. However, even with binoculars it's more or less impossible to make out the improbable trail over the next day's pass, the Colle di Valcornera, as the ground is rocky and steep.

Enjoy easy walking as the path descends slowly towards the lake. Just as you think it's going in the wrong direction (towards the dam) a left junction is reached with a signpost, and our trail turns abruptly east to enter forest. (In a little way on the left a sign shows the trail from the farm, so it must exist.)

The red larch trees provide delightful shade as you descend past a farm to emerge on the often busy highway leading from the dam along the lake. Turn left to reach the tiny hamlet of **Prarayer**.

Rifugio Prarayer

133

IBEX

Hunted throughout the Alps for its impressive horns, numbers of ibex (a goat/deer cross) were down to just 100 or so individuals by around 1820. Its heart-shaped bones were believed to be a cure-all, increasing its vulnerability. Today there are more than 15,000 ibex in the mountains of Europe, thanks largely to King Victor Emanuel of the Gran Paradiso region of Italy. A keen hunter, he foresaw an end to his sport unless something was done

to save the ibex from extinction. In the mid 19th century he established a hunting reserve in his kingdom, and thus saved the species. This reserve became the Gran Paradiso National Park in 1922, and since then the ibex has been a protected animal. All the ibex now living in the the Alps and further afield in Europe have descended from the Italian population.

A rather fine specimen

Robust and solitary, the ibex can survive the worst storms. Adept on rock, they have a predilection for abrupt slopes, grassy ledges and southern faces where they soak up the sun.

They remain at altitude throughout the year. They have ridged horns, which on a full-grown male can reach 1m in length and weigh up to 6kg. The female ibex has considerably smaller horns. The coat is beige in spring, becoming browner during the summer. Some older animals appear almost black. Their winter coat is thick, and makes them look even sturdier.

They eat at dawn and dusk, then rest during the day. The young are born in mid June, after which the mother rejoins the herd along with her offspring from the previous year. The males live in a separate herd, the oldest ones tending to live alone for the last years of their life.

Unlike the chamois, ibex do not favour the forest; they are by nature sedentary, only moving around in search of food. In the early autumn you may see male ibex fighting, standing on their hind legs and clashing horns.

The ibex are less easily spooked than the chamois, and will allow people to get reasonably close – but they do have a comfort zone, which should not be crossed.

STAGE 6
Prarayer to Breuil-Cervinia

Start	Prarayer
Access to start	Bus to Valpelline; then taxi onwards to the end of the road. Road access as far as Place Moulin next to the dam at the southwest end of the lake, 3km from Prarayer.
Altitude at start	2005m
Altitude at finish	2006m
Finish	Breuil-Cervinia
Access to finish	Bus from Aosta; road access.
Altitude gain	1180m
Altitude loss	1060m
Distance	14km
Time	9hrs
Highpoint	Colle di Valcournera 3066m
Maps	1:50,000 Istituto Geografico Centrale 5 Cervino-Matterhorn e Monte Rosa; 1:25,000 Istituto Geografico Centrale 115 La Valpelline, Valle di Ollomont, Valle di St Barthelemy
Facilities	Rifugio Perucca-Vuillermoz is very basic and does not sell any food apart from dinner and breakfast; Breuil-Cervinia has all facilities.
Transport options	Bus from Perères to Breuil-Cervinia.
Accommodation	Rifugio Prarayer; Rifugio Perucca-Vuillermoz; Breuil-Cervinia: several hotels.
Extras	Staying at the Rifugio Perucca-Vuillermoz is highly recommended to allow this stage to be enjoyed to the full. The trail emerges at the road at Perères, a few kilometres south of Cervinia. There is a regular bus service from here into town – it's worth taking it.
Escape route	There's no alternative during this stage other than to retrace your steps to Prarayer and then walk along the lake to Place Moulin and on down the valley to Valpelline. From there you can take a bus round to Breuil-Cervinia.

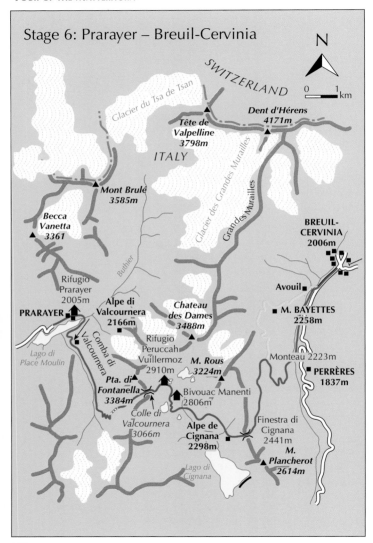

Stage 6: Prarayer – Breuil-Cervinia

N

0   1 km

SWITZERLAND

Glacier du Tsa de Tsan

Dent d'Hérens
4171m

*Tête de
Valpelline
3798m*

ITALY

Glacier des Grandes Murailles

Grandes Murailles

Mont Brulé
3585m

*Becca
Vanetta
3361*

Buthier

BREUIL-
CERVINIA
2006m

Rifugio
Prarayer
2005m

Avouil

PRARAYER

Alpe di
Valcournera
2166m

*Chateau
des Dames
3488m*

M. BAYETTES
2258m

*Lago di
Place Moulin*

*Comba di
Valcournera*

Rifugio
Peruccah
Vuillermoz
2910m

*M. Rous
3224m*

Monteau 2223m

PERRÈRES
1837m

*Pta. di
Fontanella
3384m*

Bivouac Manenti
2806m

*Colle di
Valcournera
3066m*

Alpe de
Cignana
2298m

Finestra di
Cignana
2441m

*M.
Plancherot
2614m*

*Lago di
Cignana*

Stage 6: Prarayer – Breuil-Cervinia

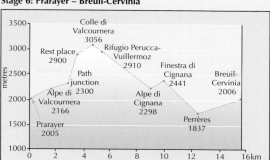

The Colle di Valcournera is a wild, rocky, often hostile place, and one of the gems of Tour of the Matterhorn. Its relative remoteness and the fact that it is not on any other established trek, nor does it provide access to any famous high peaks, gives it a unique sense of solitude and wilderness. Once the verdant green pastures of Prarayer are left behind the terrain changes quickly, and soon you are in the cold morning shade under the western slopes of the forbidding Punta di Fontanella and Monte Dragone. As you head up the Comba di Valcournera you are bound to wonder where on earth the trail can go to get out of this steep-sided valley. Zigzags and a short equipped section provide the answer, but the final slopes to the col are hard work, and often snow covered well into the summer. From the col views are extensive, all the way to the Monte Rosa summits. However, the Matterhorn remains hidden until well into the descent.

The East Face of the Colle di Valcournera is no friendlier as its angle is imposing, and again the presence of névé is likely to call for a steady step and concentration on the descent.

Once down by the Rifugio Perucca-Vuillermoz (built by local Guides in memory of two colleagues who were killed by serac fall on Liskamm during a training

137

course) everything seems much more friendly, and the surrounding blue lakes and far-off mountains provide perfect walking terrain. The hut itself is quite basic but has all necessary facilities, and Flavio the guardian will go out of his way to help and advise you.

Crags, waterfalls and lakes predominate on the descent, which leads past the little red hut Bivouac Manenti. On a sunny day this hut heats up, and it is very tempting to crawl into one of the two berths inside and take a nap. Civilisation reappears near the Lago di Cignana, to the far end of which there is road access. A chapel next to the lake is a reminder that before the valley was flooded there was a village here. Now all that remains is the small Alpe di Cignana, a summer farm. From here the trails are more frequented, being not so far from the road. The next col, Finestra di Cignana, is an exciting place because you can somehow sense that the Matterhorn must be close, but you still can't quite see it. A beautiful balcony path traverses around above flowery meadows

Looking across to Valcournera from the Comba d'Oren

and at the next shoulder there it is – the chunky profile of the Matterhorn, standing proud above the conglomeration of Breuil-Cervinia.

Breuil was the original name of the village as it was years ago, nestled at the top of the valley under the slopes of Monte Cervino, frequented since Roman times. 'Cervinia' was the name given by the fascists under Mussolini during World War II, when they wanted to destroy the long-standing Francophile culture of the Aosta region. The Valdôtain people refused this attempted reversal of their culture and took up arms, retreating to the hills and waging a war of resistance.

After the liberation most places resumed their French names, but at Breuil-Cervinia they kept both – presumably the incorporation of the Italian name for the Matterhorn, Cervino, was regarded as a good tourist attraction.

Breuil-Cervinia is a fairly typical resort town with a mix of old and new. The church sports a rather fine sundial and there are some attractive houses, but do not expect to be bowled over by the architecture in general. However, the presence of the Matterhorn is probably enough to warrant a night here, along with a final appreciation of Italian cuisine, beverages and hospitality.

ROUTE

About 200m beyond Prarayer, towards the Refuge Aosta, a path heads off right, signed to the 'Oratories de Cuney'. Just below, a bridge over the river gives access to forest, and after a short way the path reaches a junction where trail number 12 goes left and number 13 goes right. Number 12 is the one for us; it's also labelled number 3 in a triangle denoting that it is an *alta via* (high route) number 3. The trail takes well-graded zigzags up through the forest to the treeline where a newly constructed *alpage* is soon passed, and the trail continues along a very old track that heads up into the valley. In the morning it is cold in the shade of the mountains, and all around are rocky faces and boulder slopes. Behind are the sunny slopes of yesterday's descent, a marked contrast to this morning's terrain.

This exciting stage of the trek takes you from Prarayer, nestled away in the high mountains, over yet another high pass to reach the Valtournanche and the Italian face of the Matterhorn.

Enjoy this rare flat walking – it doesn't last long! The Colle di Valcournera is way up on the left, and a very obvious boulder with a painted sign marks where you must leave the gentle mule track and head up the improbable slopes above. Cairns do go straight on up the valley, but where to I do not know.

The zigzagged path is steep but well graded and height is soon gained, especially on the section which is equipped with a very easy via ferrata of rungs and chains. Views around are opening up now but the best are those behind, down to the lake and up the Comba d'Oren that you descended the day before. After a long climb a flat area is finally reached, and a break is definitely deserved here. Best not to study what's to come as it's a formidable boulder slope, equally as steep as what has gone before but without the nice switchbacks. There are at least three different paths heading up this slope, and you'll probably end up using parts of all of them.

To reach the slope you have to wend your way through rocks; keep a careful watch for the waymarks so

It's a bit of a slog to reach the Colle di Valcournera

The Rifugio Perrucca-Vuillermoz in morning sun, with Colle di Valcournera behind

as to find the easiest passage. After this – as you embark on the final slope – be careful not to veer too far left; try to stay in the middle of the slope where possible. If snow remains from the summer bear in mind that it could still be frozen and thus icy and slippery.

After this final grind it will be with great relief that you'll reach the **Colle di Valcournera** (3066m) with its wooden cross. Take a break and enjoy the views of the far-off peaks and nearby lakes. The Rifugio Perrucca-Vuillermoz is just below at 2910m, with the deep blue waters of the Lago del Dragone nearby. Look closely at the col as you may find some unusual wild flowers here, including the rare King of the Alps if you're lucky.

Once rested it's time to get on with the descent. The path heads to the right (south) at first, then straight down. Care needs to be taken as the initial section is rather steep, and often still snowy from the winter. Hopefully any snow will be soft and melting on this East Face by the time you arrive, but on cloudy days névé often

Passing the tiny Bivouac Manenti on the descent from the Rifugio Perrucca-Vuillermoz

stays hard all day. Fresh snow is also a possibility late in the season. An ice axe – or at least trekking poles – and crampons could be useful here. Whilst the lower slopes in snow could be glissaded at the top, it's necessary to keep in control as it's too far and too steep to slide safely all the way. In snowfree conditions the initial descent is still quite intimidating, and the moraine too unstable to allow a good track to be constructed – efforts have been made, but there is a still a short section where you just have to stumble down as best you can. Usually there is a handline down the first part of the path, then where the path is eroded away there is a bolt, so if conditions were really bad presumably you could tie a rope to this.

Things soon ease up and you can relax as you amble down a beautifully made track, bordered by large stones, to quickly reach the **Rifugio Perucca-Vuillermoz**, perched on a wonderful vantage point. The lake below, dominated by Mont Dragone, is surrounded by granite slabs, set at a perfect angle for sunbathing – why resist? In the evening ibex often roam near the hut and it's fantastic to watch the sun setting far away in the valleys. Later the twinkling lights of the towns make you realise how high up you are.

The path leaves the hut and traverses rocks below with the help of some chains before reaching the delightful little red **Bivouac Manenti**, a really nice warm place to sit and admire the surrounding cliffs and lakes. The trail passes a cave in the cliffs, which would provide a good shelter from rain (but not a storm), before continuing down past a beautiful cascading waterfall to a flat viewpoint by a big cairn. Ahead the artificial Lago di Cignana is visible, which has nearby road access so many people come up from there to walk. At the **Alpe di Cignana** follow the track, but look out for a grassy path going off left into the meadows and climb briefly to the small pass **Finestra di Cignana** (2441m). From here a beckoning small trail goes directly up the neighbouring summit of Mont Pancherot (2614m); the summit is reached in 50mins (according to the sign). This would be a good extra for those not too desperate to see the Matterhorn, which soon comes into view – just follow the path around the next shoulder and there it is!

Descending to the Lago di Cignana

143

For the rest of the descent to Breuil-Cervinia these early views of the peak from the Italian side can be enjoyed. The route continues as a traverse, followed by zigzags through meadows, then descends into larch forest to a junction at **Monteau** where route number 3 is directed left and upwards (see variant below). The main trail continues down through pastures past a water source to a strange open area of earthworks, where there is a water fountain. Walk back into the woods to descend to a bridge and the road at **Perrères**.

There is a bus service from Perrères to Breuil-Cervinia, and it can be good to take this if the fleshpots are calling. It is of course tempting to walk all the way into town – but don't say you haven't been warned: the first part of the path along the river is not the most salubrious of places, and gives an insight into some of the horrible things produced by a holiday resort. So, to walk into town take the path signed number 107 which goes left just after the bridge. Wander along next to the river, avoiding some rather suspicious pipes belching out indescribable debris. Later, after passing a lake, the trail is much more pleasant, and you soon arrive on the main road again to walk the last few metres up into **Breuil-Cervinia**.

VARIANT

A high-level variant goes off the main route from Monteau, signed trail number 3. This could be an alternative way into Breuil-Cervinia if you have the time, and is far better than the regular way next to the river. However, the path is somewhat overgrown by alder bushes, and whilst the ascent is short, pushing through the vegetation in the afternoon heat is quite tedious. Once out of the bushes the high path is excellent. You can leave it at an obvious junction with a path which takes you down to join the river path at a lake. From here the track into Breuil-Cervinia is fine.

THE BREITHORN

The Tour of the Matterhorn takes you very near to the Breithorn peak, and an ascent is perfectly feasible as a conclusion to the tour on Stage 7. 'Wide mountain' would be the literal translation, and it fits this summit well: the Breithorn stretches well over 2km from its main western summit to the eastern one. Its huge bulk towers above Zermatt, and can be seen when coming up the Mattertal well before the Matterhorn deigns to show itself.

A beautiful morning on the way to the Breithorn (Stage 7 variant)

At 4164m the Breithorn is not the highest peak in the area, but it must be the most climbed due to its accessibility from the Klein Matterhorn lift and the relative ease of the ascent from the south side. It is the most westerly peak of the giants rising up from the Gorner Glacier. The Breithorn actually has four summits: the westerly highpoint, the central summit (4160m), the eastern summit (4141m) and Roccia Nera (4075m) which – as its name suggests – is a rocky summit above the Schwarztor col, separating it from Pollux.

The North Face is steep, complex and avalanche prone, and when viewed from that side it seems an impossible challenge to those aspirant climbers who ascend this as their first 4000m peak. In total contrast the southern side presents a gentle snow slope which allows the ascent to be achieved in about 3hrs from the cable car. The Breithorn was first climbed by this route in 1813 when it was somewhat more of an endeavour without the aid of lifts. From Italy the Testa Grigia lift gives convenient access, but this entails an hour's more climbing than the ultimate short day out from the Klein Matterhorn.

If you choose to include the ascent of the Breithorn in your Tour of the Matterhorn be prepared to see people in all sorts of gear, ranging from ultra-cool latest fashion designer shoes and jeans and T-shirts to people walking the dog to well-equipped mountaineers. You'll probably also see people on skis going up. Do not be put off by the unroped folk who look like they've just nipped up in between shopping in Zermatt. This is a glacier and there are crevasses. You do need to be roped up for the ascent, and you will almost certainly need to use crampons. Take a Guide if you are not versed in glacier-travel techniques. Whilst the ascent seems pretty innocuous in sunny weather and good snow conditions, it is a whole different ball game in fog when navigation can be very difficult. The deaths of five ski tourers here in 1977 reminds one of the dangers. Don't forget too that the Breithorn rises to 4164m; for many people this will be the first time they have reached that altitude. The symptoms of High Mountain Sickness are often not registered until it is too late.

At any time during the summer there will be lots of guided groups, as the Breithorn is bread-and-butter work for the Guides from Zermatt and Breuil-Cervinia and they do an excellent job. A guided ascent will not only keep you safe but the Guide will also be able to tell you about all the surrounding peaks that can be seen from here. It is truly a 360-degree panorama: from the Matterhorn to the Dent Blanche to the Obergabelhorn, the Zinal Rothorn and the Weisshorn guarding the Mattertal, to the Dom and the Täschhorn and the Monte Rosa massif. Nearer are the twin peaks of Pollux and Castor, and far away in the mist the distant Italian plains.

On the summit of the Breithorn

STAGE 7
Breuil-Cervinia to Zermatt

Start	Breuil-Cervinia
Access to start	Bus from Aosta; road access.
Altitude at start	2006m
Finish	Zermatt
Access to finish	Train from Visp; bus and road access to Täsch; then train to Zermatt.
Altitude at finish	1600m
Altitude gain	(Breuil-Cervinia to the Theodulpass) 1295m
Altitude loss	1720m
Distance	19km
Time	9+hrs
Highpoint	Theodulpass 3301m or Plateau Rosa/Testa Grigia 3479m
Maps	1:50,000 Istituto Geografico Centrale 5 Cervino-Matterhorn e Monte; Rosa Carte Nationale de la Suisse 5006 Matterhorn Mischabel; 1:25,000 Istituto Geografico Centrale 108 Cervino Matterhorn, Breuil Cervinia, Champoluc; Carte Nationale de la Suisse 1348 Zermatt
Facilities	The Theodulhütte and the Rifugio Guide del Cervino offer snacks and a restaurant service. Gandegghütte has an excellent menu. There is a café at Trocknersteg and several at Furi.
Transport options	Cable car from Breuil-Cervinia to Plateau Rosa/Testa Grigia; cable car from Trocknersteg to Furi; cable car from Furi to Zermatt.
Accommodation	Breuil-Cervinia: several hotels; Theodulhütte; Testa Grigia: Rifugio Guide del Cervino; Gandegghütte; Zermatt: lots of hotels.
Extras	This stage can be walked in its entirety, or any – or all – of the available lifts can be used. You can decide depending on energy levels, tolerance to walking beneath functioning lifts,

the state of the bank balance, time available and impatience to get Zermatt. All parts of the walk have their attraction

Escape route   If you have to abandon the trek at Breuil-Cervinia the quickest way back to Zermatt is to take the Plateau Rosa cable car then either walk up to the Klein Matterhorn cable car or descend to Trocknersteg. If conditions mean that walking is not possible then you will have to take transport from Breuil-Cervinia to Zermatt, but it's a very long way: Chatillon–Aosta–Gran St Bernard–Martigny–Visp–Zermatt.

Monte Cervino   The final stage of this exciting journey around the Matterhorn leads us once again away from the grassy meadows and waymarked footpaths up into the high mountain world of snow and glaciers, ice faces and crevasses. It matters not whether you choose to add on an ascent of the Breithorn – just making the passage from Italy to Switzerland is an exploit in itself.

The journey from the Valtournanche to the Mattertal is one filled with history and apprehension – a venture that would have struck fear into the hearts of travellers of old as they prepared to face the rigours and unknown terrors of the high mountains. Nowadays ski lifts and bulldozed pistes have tamed these wild mountains. In winter skiers based in Zermatt and Cervinia frequently ski from one side to the other to have lunch, enjoying a few more runs down the beautifully groomed pistes before returning to their holiday base.

In the summer it's a slightly different story. The choice is to walk up to the Theodulpass (3301m) or to take the lifts from Breuil-Cervinia to the Plateau Rosa (3479m). Having taken the lifts on many occasions I eventually decided to walk from town up to the historic Theodulpass – I was keen to step in the footsteps of the ancients. I saw on the map that there was an old chapel (Capelle Bontadini) en route, where travellers would pray for protection from the elements before embarking on the final stage of their climb. Sadly I was disappointed. This area is an example of the worst ravages of winter tourism – lifts abound, along with the associated junk and destruction of the slopes – and the chapel was almost hidden, squashed between two ski-lift buildings, and now used as a storeroom for rescue equipment! However, I am glad I have walked it; maybe some walkers will feel the same and, forewarned, will not be too appalled. Whether or not walking is possible also depends on the amount of snow remaining here after the winter – I have arrived in July to find summer skiing (which operates on the glaciated slopes of the Zermatt side of the massif) also open from the Plan Maison lift above Breuil-Cervinia. In this case walking is certainly not an option!

The walk up leads to the Theodulpass; if you take the lift you will arrive at Testa Grigia. The whole area is known as the Plateau Rosa, and the two cols are just 15–30mins' walk apart. There is a hut on each one. Staying there allows you to savour the mountain scenery and to spend a night up amongst the glaciers. It also means that in the morning the descent of the Theodule Glacier

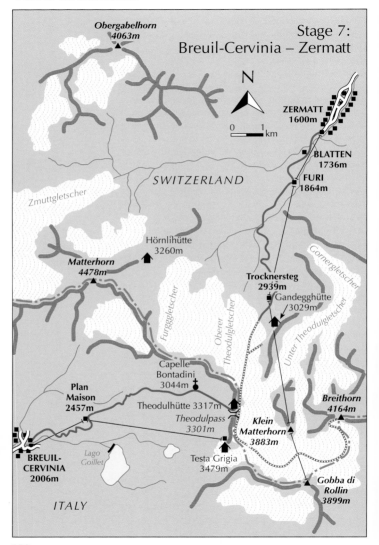

Stage 7:
Breuil-Cervinia – Zermatt

N

0   1
└────────┘
km

Obergabelhorn
4063m

Zermatt
1600m

BLATTEN
1736m

FURI
1864m

SWITZERLAND

Zmuttgletscher

Hörnlihütte
3260m

Gornergletscher

Matterhorn
4478m

Trocknersteg
2939m

Gandegghütte
3029m

Furggletscher

Oberer
Theodulgletscher

Unter Theodulgletscher

Capelle
Bontadini
3044m

Plan
Maison
2457m

Theodulhütte 3317m

Theodulpass
3301m

Klein
Matterhorn
3883m

Breithorn
4164m

BREUIL-
CERVINIA
2006m

Lago
Goillet

Testa Grigia
3479m

Gobba di
Rollin
3899m

ITALY

could be icy and crampons might be needed, but you will avoid late-in-the-day slushy conditions which can be very wet and soggy, not to mention a bit dangerous on this snow slope. Anyone wishing to extend the trek to the top of the Breithorn will have to stay at one of the huts.

The descent of the Oberer Theodule Glacier is not long (1–1hr 30mins), and you will doubtless see a whole mix of people, from skiers and snowboarders to runners in shorts and people in training shoes with dogs – and fully equipped mountaineers. The deal is that this is a glacier and it is crevassed; I have seen the crevasses and seen people fall in them. You need to be roped if there is any fresh snow on this glacier. In lean conditions, or near the end of the season, the slope becomes quite a mess near the bottom. The ski-piste machines try to keep it groomed for the whole summer, and their passage back and forth at the bottom makes it look more like a building site than a mountain snow slope. The scene of devastation around the Trocknersteg lift station is a disgrace.

The best plan is to leave the glacier at about 3100m and head right (east) to the rocky ridge on which, just to the north, is situated the delightful Gandegg restaurant. You will avoid the dirty snow at the end of the glacier,

Stage 7: Breuil-Cervinia – Zermatt

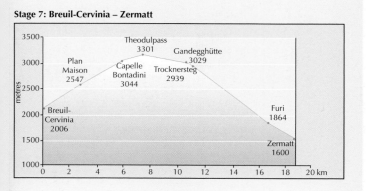

151

The gentle glaciated slopes of the Breithorn's South Face

and Gandegg provides one of the most fantastic panoramas around Zermatt. From here you can see many, if not all, of the high Zermatt peaks: the stunning North Face of the Breithorn, Pollux, Castor, Liskamm with its elegant arêtes, and the multiple summits of the Monte Rosa massif. Below the Gornergletscher snakes down past the Rifflehorn; to the west is the Matterhorn, as well as the Obergabelhorn and the Weisshorn, among others. This is a fantastic place to stop and eat rösti whilst savouring this awe-inspiring scenery. Despite the invasion of ski lifts and the consequent infrastructure that goes with such major tourist development, the peaks here are quite splendid – and nothing can change that.

Depending on time and the desire to hit town, I do recommend walking down to Zermatt, at least from Furi and ideally from Trocknersteg. Once away from the Trocknersteg lift station the walk is very pleasant and largely on footpaths, not pistes. Don't miss the stretch from Furi down to Zermatt, as it offers a couple of path options down through the larch forests amongst ancient blackened wood chalets, maybe visiting Blatten, birthplace of famous Guide Ulrich Inderbinen, before emerging into the madness of Zermatt.

Flags at the Theodulhütte: Italian, Swiss and the Valle d'Aosta

The journey from the grassy meadows of Breuil-Cervinia to the wooden chalets of Zermatt involves crossing the loftiest mountain pass on the trek amidst the spectacular glaciers of the high mountains.

ROUTE

From Breuil-Cervinia the cable car to Plan Maison is clearly signed. If walking, take path number 15, signed just before the lift on the left. It gives 1hr 40mins to Plan Maison. The path winds up through meadows past chalets, first to the left of the lift, then traverses underneath and continues to climb more or less following the line of the cables to **Plan Maison** lift station.

Views of the Matterhorn are excellent from here and all the way onwards, but there are a multitude of other lesser-known summits to admire too, such as the Dent d'Hérens, the Punta Margherita, and a whole series of rocky peaks running south from here. Ahead and east are the Plateau Rosa and Testa Grigia, and further right the Ventina Glacier, which tumbles down from the Gobba di Rollin.

From Plan Maison either take the cable car to the Testa Grigia or follow path 15 which is signed to the Theodulpass in 2hrs 15mins. This takes off straight towards the pass and is generally signed by yellow arrows all the way, but they can be hard to spot (especially if there is névé around). To begin with routefinding presents no problems and you climb fairly quickly up past a track going off left to a café. At the next junction it's gentler to go left rather than following the jeep track which doesn't zigzag. Continuing on, the trail arrives at two ski-lift stations, named for their respective altitudes: Plan Maison 2866 and Plan Maison 2876. There are ugly snow cannons here, which never look their best in the summer. According to the Italian map the path goes up to the right of the lifts, but in reality it goes to the left. However, it doesn't really matter which way you go – in fog you would just follow the lift cables to reach the next lift station, **Bontadini**. A path comes in from the right here: the Tour of Monte Rosa coming over from the Colle del Cime Bianche. Bontadini was an Italian Alpinist and there is a memorial plaque for him in the tiny chapel sandwiched between the lift buildings – a delightful juxtaposition of old and new. An information board starts with the words 'The landscape in front of you wasn't always as you see it today...' Too true! Presumably this is where travellers stopped to pray for protection before tackling the final climb to the pass; now it's a storehouse. Try hard and you might get an inkling of how those travellers of old felt here...

The Tour of Monte Rosa joins the Tour of the Matterhorn from here on to Zermatt, and the signpost gives 45mins to the Theodulpass. As you continue the climb a pointed snowy peak appears on the other side of the pass – the Breithorn.

The yellow waymarks are rather sparse and difficult to follow. Basically the path sets off from the left side of the upper lift, signed 15 and TMR, then goes over right. The shiny metal Theodulhütte can be seen, with a wire fence around it. If you lose the yellow waymarks then just take the best way to this – there are numerous paths, flashed in various colours. Look out for a wide track, which goes right then winds up past an iron cross. There is then a small path to the right, just after a bend to the left, which leads up to the hut. Another route comes in from the left, so don't be too surprised if your route does not match mine exactly. In fog it may be wise to take the cable car, as this area is very confusing and it helps to be able to see the hut to get your bearings. You

From the Gandegghütte you can enjoy fabulous views of the glaciated peaks above the Gornergletscher

will arrive directly at the hut, which is just above the Theodulpass.

The **Theodulhütte** is an old building clad in metal sheeting. Inside it has a more traditional feel – as well as the original part there is also a new big dining room which juts out over the pass with good views down to Italy.

If you take the cable car to **Testa Grigia** you need to walk to the hut. Follow the ski lift down, then cut left (usually signed to the hut) and pass just under a rocky bluff with a number of pylons on it. Go down to the **Theodulpass** then up a few metres to the hut. It takes about 20mins and the hut is visible all the way. Alternatively stay at the **Rifugio Guide del Cervino**.

To continue on to Zermatt you must next descend from the **Theodulpass** via the **Oberer Theodule Glacier**. Do not be influenced by what other people are doing; if there is any fresh snow at all you should rope up for this descent. Follow the ski piste next to the T-bar lift, keeping well to the edge of the piste and taking the best terrain. Conditions vary hugely during the summer, from firm white snow to slush to hard ice to dirty melting channels

VARIANT

If you're looking to do a glaciated summit during the trek then the Breithorn (4164m) is the obvious candidate. It is located not far from the Plateau Rosa and can be attempted after a night spent here or at the Theodulhütte. However, this is a high Alpine peak, and despite its proximity to the lifts is a serious proposition. You must be experienced in glacier travel and the use of crampons and ice axe. The weather can change very quickly at this altitude, and during storms conditions become very serious at 4000m. Unless you have already climbed such peaks it is strongly recommended that you take a Guide to do this ascent. Guides can be hired from Zermatt, Breuil-Cervinia or directly at the Rifugio Guide del Cervino or the Theodulhütte.

filled with grit. Do not hesitate to use crampons if necessary. To the left is the omnipresent Matterhorn, whilst up ahead is the Mattertal Valley flanked by the Dom and the Täschhorn to the right (east) and the Weisshorn, Obergabelhorn and Zinal Rothorn to the west. After about 1hr of descent, at about 3100m, head over to the true right bank of the glacier to get onto the rocky ridge that gives access to Gandegg (3029m) – you can see the flag for Gandegg from the glacier. This avoids having to descend the often slushy and dirty lower part of the glacier and also leads you to lunch at the restaurant. The **Gandegghütte** is a regular mountain hut, so if you do not feel ready to leave the mountains yet you could spend a last night here.

After a pleasant break savouring this splendid viewpoint follow a red waymarked path for about 10mins to the rather less-than-splendid lift station at **Trockensteg**. If time is short, or you've had your fill of walking, take the cable car to Furi. If not find the footpath which leaves the lift station to the right (east). The signpost gives a time of 2hrs 30mins to Zermatt. The path winds down among rocks, well marked in red and white, then heads across left under the cable car. It continues to descend, less well marked now, until it reaches grassy ground. Views of the Obergabelhorn, Weisshorn and Zinal Rothorn are particularly fine from here, as well as the long Gornergletscher snaking down to Zermatt. A sign is reached for 'Furgg, Schwarzee' one way and 'Furi, Zermatt' the other – this latter path descends next to the river to another sign, indicating 'Hermetje' to the left and 'Furi, Zermatt' right. The latter uses the ski piste to descend so it's rough underfoot but reasonably direct, and the small settlement of **Furi** is soon reached. Several restaurants offer a tempting break before the last part of the descent to Zermatt.

The whole way is signed and within sight of Zermatt, and takes about 1hr. I recommend going via **Blatten**, the village where Ulrich Inderbinen was raised. You can see the boulder where he and his sister learned to climb, and the village's gleaming white chapel has been beautifully renovated. From here down to Zermatt is but a stroll down an easy track, and brings you out onto the high street.

ULRICH INDERBINEN

Born in Zermatt at the dawn of the 20th century to a poor farming family, Ulrich Inderbinen was not only a legendary Alpine Guide, he was also the oldest Guide in the region. For 70 years he guided clients up the local 4000m peaks. He lost count of the number of times he climbed the Matterhorn, but always remembered his first ascent, when he was 21.

He had decided that farming was too hard a way to earn a living and that he would prefer to guide in the mountains; he needed climbing experience, so enlisted his sister and two friends as partners. From

his summer village home in Blatten Ulrich had a perfect view of the Matterhorn and was able to study the summit. In his back yard there was a handy boulder on which he and his siblings honed their climbing skills. Equipped with only the most basic gear the group of four successfully reached the summit. Ulrich was to concede later that it was extremely perilous, as they had to carry flickering candle lanterns and to find the route by searching for scratch marks left on the rocks by previous parties. From thereon he made his living as a Guide, although this was not an easy profession in the war years when tourists were thin on the ground.

The monument to Ulrich Inderbinen

Ulrich eventually became an institution in Zermatt. Much sought-after as a Guide, especially later in his life when his fund of stories was unique, Ulrich could be found outside the church each evening. He was proud to be the only resident in town with no telephone. He took up competitive skiing at 80, and always won in his category. His relentless Alpine plod left many a younger person gasping for breath, and he was still climbing mountains in his nineties. Ulrich died in June 2004 at the age of 103.

APPENDIX I:
Further Reading

There are masses of books about Zermatt and the Matterhorn, but the following are good to read and provide lots of information.

Zermatt Saga by Cicely Williams (Roten-Verlag, 1989) is an account of Zermatt from the year dot by the wife of the Bishop of the English Church in Zermatt in the 1960s. Mrs Williams spent time in Zermatt since childhood and is clearly in love with the place. Whilst her description of life there in the present day is rather dated, her history is spot on, and the book gives an insight to what can only be described as a bygone age.

How the English made the Alps by Jim Ring (John Murray, 2000) is a broad account of the activities of English mountaineers throughout the Alps. Many first ascents of Alpine peaks were made by local Guides with English clients, and this book is an easy and interesting read.

The High Mountains of the Alps by Helmut Dumler and Willi Burkhardt (Diadem, 1994) is the bible for all those who dream of ascending these giants; the photos alone will provide more than enough inspiration.

Scrambles amongst the Alps by Edward Whymper (National Geographic, 2002) provides the first-hand account of the fateful first ascent of the Matterhorn, as well as many more detailed accounts of climbing during the 1860s.

Ulrich Inderbinen: As old as the century by Heidi Lanz and Liliane De Meester (Roten-Verlag, 1997) tells Ulrich Inderbinen's story of growing up and becoming a Guide in Zermatt.

Our Alpine Flora by the Swiss Alpine Club (SAC, 1989) will fund many hours of research in the evenings as you try to figure out what 'those flowers' are.

Le Tour du Cervin is a superb picture book of the trek, in French, by Mario Colonel.

The Trek Atlas (New Holland, 2006) is another coffee-table book featuring many treks, worldwide, including the Tour of the Matterhorn.

APPENDIX II
Accommodation

Stage 1
Zermatt Hotels
Ottovan Täschalp Europaweghütte tel: 027 967 2301; fax: 027 966 3965; email: Willischthomas@yahoo.com www.europahuette.ch
Europahütte Fam Marcel Brantschen, tel (hut): 027 967 8247; tel (private, ie to contact the guardian when the hut is closed): 027 967 8278; fax: 027 967 6074; mobile: 079 291 3322; email: fam.brantschen.europahuette@freesurf.ch
Grächen Hotels
St Niklaus Hotels
Stage 2
Jungu Pension Jägerstübli, tel: 027 956 21 01; mobile: 078 606 2528
Topalihütte tel: 027 956 2172; mobile: 079 220 4006; email: www.topalihitta. ch. albrecht.reto@bluewin.ch
Gruben-Meiden Hotel Schwarzhorn, tel: 027 932 1414
Stage 3
Hotel Weisshorn tel: 027 475 1106
Zinal Hotels, Auberge Alpina, tel: 027 475 1224; fax: 027 475 5033
Stage 4
Moiry barrage tel (restaurant): 027 475 1548; tel (private – when hut closed): 027 475 1081; mobile: 079 471 8051; email: clems@bluewin.ch
Cabane de Moiry tel (hut): 027 475 4534
Les Haudères Hotels
Stage 5
Arolla Hotels
Rifugio Collon-Nacamuli tel: 0165 730047
Prarayer tel: 0165 730040/730922
Stage 6
Rifugio Perucca-Vuillermoz Flavio Bich, tel: 338 4264705
Breuil-Cervinia Hotels
Stage 7
Albergo Plan Maison
Testa Grigia – Rifugio Guide del Cervino Fam Antonio Carrel, tel: 0166 948369; fax: 0166 93129; email: giorgiocarrel@galactica.it
Theodulhütte tel: 0166 949400; mobile: 338 326 7009
Gandegghütte Gervas Perren, tel: 027 967 2112; fax: 027 967 2149; mobile: 079 607 8868; email: gandegghuette@holidaynet.ch

APPENDIX III
Useful Contacts

Tourist Offices

All phone numbers are noted in the form used when phoning from within the respective country. When phoning from elsewhere add the country code and change the numbers accordingly: to call a Swiss number from outside Switzerland dial the international code (in Europe usually 00), then drop the first zero of the number; to call an Italian number from outside Italy dial the international code, then the number in its entirety.

Tourist Office Zermatt tel: 027 966 8100; fax: 027 966 8101; www.zermatt.ch zermatt@wallis.ch

Tourist Office Täsch tel: 027 967 1689; fax: 027 967 2118; www.taesch.ch info@taesch.ch

Tourist Office Randa tel: 027 967 1677; fax: 027 967 1679; www.randa.ch tourismus@randa.ch

Tourist Office Grächen tel: 027 955 6060; fax: 027 955 6066; www.graechen.ch info@graechen.ch

Tourist Office St Niklaus tel: 027 956 3663; fax: 027 956 2925; www.st-niklaus.ch info@st-niklaus.ch

Tourist Office Turtmanntal tel: 027 932 1691; fax: 027 932 3784; www.turtmanntal.ch info@turtmann-turtmanntal.ch

Tourist Office Zinal tel: 027 475 1370; fax: 027 475 2977; www.zinal.ch zinal@sierre-anniviers.ch

Tourist Office Les Haudères tel: 027 283 1015; fax: 027 283 1053; www.evolene-region.ch les haudures@evolene-region.ch

Tourist Office Arolla tel: 027 283 1083; fax: 027 283 2270; www.arolla.ch arolla@span.ch

Tourist Office Breuil-Cervinia tel: 0166 949136; fax: 0166 949731; www.montecervino.it breuil-cervinia@montecervino.net

Aosta region www.regione.vda.it

Guides' Offices
Zermatt tel: 027 966 0101

Breuil-Cervinia tel: 0166 948169; fax: 0166 949885; www.guidedelcervino.com

Gear Shop
You will probably have all the gear you need when you arrive in the Alps, but you may need to buy maps, guidebooks, or extra equipment before or during the trek. Zermatt has a vast range of sports shops stocking everything you might (or might not) ever need for the mountains. Maps can be bought from the Wega bookshop, which is on the high street opposite the turn-off to the post office. Elsewhere en route there are gear shops in Les Haudères, Arolla and Breuil-Cervinia.

APPENDIX IV:
Useful Terms and Glossary

Alpage Summer farm used in the process of transhumance (see below).

Bisse Man-made waterway or irrigation channel.

Col Pass or saddle; in German usually *joch*; in Italian *colle* or *bocca*.

Cwm/corrie/combe Basin bordered on three sides by hills or mountains, either steep sided or more gently rounded. Often holds a lake, with a stream flowing out of the unenclosed side down into the valley.

Tal Valley; as in Mattertal, Turtmanntal, and so on.

Transhumance Process of farming in the Alps whereby animals are taken to graze the higher meadows during the summer months.

Weather			
English	**French**	**Italian**	**German**
weather	temps	tempo	wetter
forecast	prévision	bolletino	vohersage (wetter)
hot	chaud	caldo	heiss
cold	froid	freddo	kalt
sunny	ensoleillé	soleggiato	sonnig
rainy	pluvieux	piovos	regnerisch
windy	venté	ventoso	windig
cloudy	nuageux	nuvoloso	bewölkt
foggy	brouillard	nebbioso	neblig
stormy	orageux	temporalesco	stürmisch
snowy	enneigé	nevoso	schneereich
temperature	température	temperatura	temperatur
changeable	variable	variabile	veränderlich verschneit
thunder	tonnère	tuono	donner
lightning	éclair	fulmine	blitz
gusts/gales	rafales	raffiche di vento	bö, windstoss
white out	jour blanc	luce abbacinante	verlieren der sicht
ice	glace	ghiaccio	eis
verglace	verglas	ghiaccio vivo, verglace	glatteis

hail	grêle	grandine	hagel
avalanche	avalanche	valanga	lawine
freezing	glacial	congelamento	eisig, eiskalt
starry	étoilé	stellato	sternklar

Emergency

Help!	au secours!	aiuto!	hilfe
Accident	accident	incidente	unfall
Emergency	urgence	emergenza	notfall
Stop!	halte	stop (alt)	stop
Quick	vite	presto	schnell
Be careful!	faites attention	attenzione	achtung
Rescue	secours	soccorso	retten, rettung
Helicopter	hélicoptère	elicottero	hubschrauber Am-
bulance	ambulance	ambulanza	ambulanz
Hospital	hôpital	ospedale	spital
Doctor	medecin/docteur	dottore, medico	doktor, arzt
SOS telephone	téléphone d'urgence	telefono di soccorso	nottelefon
Heart attack	crise cardiaque	attacco di cuore, infarto	herzanfall
Stroke	hémiplégie	attacco	schlaganfall
Broken arm/leg	bras/jambe cassé(e)	braccio rotto, gamba rotta	armbruch
Asthma attack	crise d'asthma	attacco d'asma	asthmaanfall

APPENDIX V
Glacier Travel and Crevasse Rescue Techniques

Adapted from *Snowshoeing: Mont Blanc and the Western Alps* by Hilary Sharp.
The principal hazard of glacier travel is that of hidden crevasses. On a dry glacier
(ie a glacier not covered with snow) crevasses are obvious and therefore pose
no problems. However, on a wet (snow-covered) glacier what lurks beneath the
surface presents a very real danger.

Travel therefore on a wet glacier is always undertaken roped together – even
if there is a good track and good visibility. Roping up wrongly and/or using the
rope incorrectly can make any crevasse incident worse. It is therefore essential
to adopt correct practise and to keep to certain guidelines. This guide is not in-
tended as an instruction manual, and what follows is more of a reminder. Glacier
travel and crevasse rescue techniques must be learnt and practised, either on a
specialised course or from an experienced mountaineer or a professional.

Each participant should be equipped with the minimum of an ice axe, a
harness and screwgate krab, an ice screw, a 120cm sling, three prussik loops,
a pulley and three spare karabiners. The party should have a dynamic rope, the
minimum diameter of which should be 8mm, though in practise a larger diameter
is more user-friendly when it comes to handling in a crevasse rescue situation.
It is not necessary to have a designated *single* rope of 10 or 11mm if only pure
glacier travel is envisaged. The minimum length should be about 30m for two
people. For larger numbers a longer rope or two ropes should be used.

We will look at glacier travel for a party of two people. The walkers should
be roped together with about 10m of rope between them (see Figure 1). To do
this each should tie into the ends of the rope and take an equal number of coils
around their shoulders until the middle 10m is left. The coils are tied off by passing a bight of rope around them and tying an overhand knot around the rope that
leads between the walkers. This leaves a loop, which can be clipped back into
the harness with the screwgate karabiner.

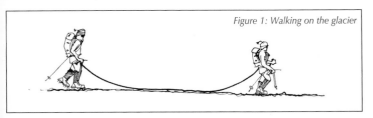

Figure 1: Walking on the glacier

When walking the rope should be kept reasonably tight – so that the middle 5–6m glide along the snow. If this tension is maintained, not only will the rope be kept away from sharp crampons, it also avoids the dangerous practise of holding the rope up in your hand, the result of which can be a serious shoulder injury in the event of a crevasse fall.

One trekking pole should be stowed away on the rucksack leaving that hand free for the ice axe. The axe MUST be instantly available for arresting a fall, not attached to the back of the rucksack. It should be carried by the head, with the shaft downwards like a walking stick, in the uphill hand whenever appropriate.

Two further refinements of this basic system are the pre-attachment of prussik loops to the rope and the tying of knots in the rope at intervals along the 10m. The theory behind the latter method is that in the event of a crevasse fall the rope will cut into the snow lip and the knot will jam into the snow, thus arresting the fall. The downside of this system is that if the snow is very soft the knot will pass right through the snow and will hinder the consequent rescue.

It is worth considering putting the lightest person at the front as disparity in weight is an important factor, but bear in mind that it's not always the first person to cross that breaks a fragile snowbridge.

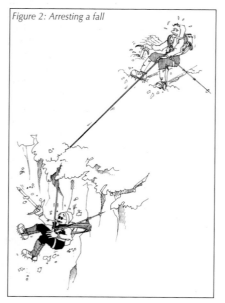

Figure 2: Arresting a fall

Although both members of the party should be vigilant at all times on a glacier, some particularly crevassed areas will obviously be more dangerous than others. This information should be passed back from the leader so that the second person can prepare himself and tighten the rope further.

The first reaction to one of the walkers falling into a crevasse can determine success or failure. If the other person is pulled flat on his face then arresting the fall becomes very difficult. The ideal reaction is to jerk backwards and adopt a semi-sitting position, with the shaft of the axe plunged into the snow (see Figure 2).

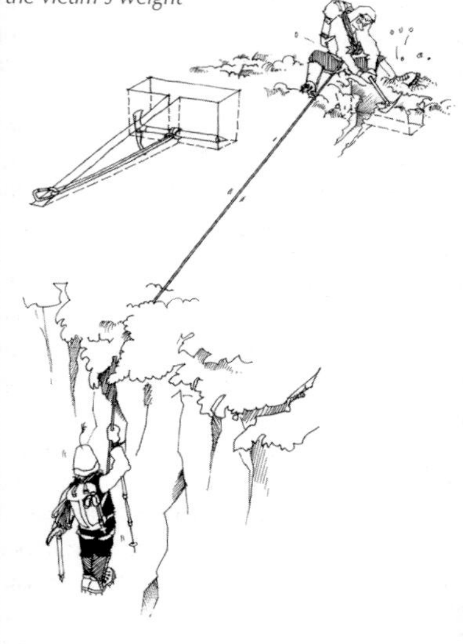

Figure 3: Constructing a belay and transferring the victim's weight

Before doing anything else the rescuer should:

1 Shout to try to make contact with the victim – it may well be that by lowering him slightly he will be able to walk out of the crevasse on the other side.

2 Look around for other people. A group of 4–5 will be able to use brute force to pull the victim up or, at worst, help in the following stages of the rescue.

3 Ascertain whether it's possible for the victim to ascend the rope using his prussik loops, assuming he knows how to do this.

The basic belay for crevasse rescue in snow is the horizontally buried ice axe (if the snow isn't deep enough then this is where the ice screw comes in). A slot must first be cut, using the axe, at right angles to the pull of the rope and as deep as possible. It should be the length of the axe and the forward wall should be slightly incut to avoid the axe being pulled out. A second slot, this time in line with the pull, should be cut, thus forming a T. It must be the same depth as the first slot and should rise to the surface at as shallow an angle as possible. Doing this is not easy and is further hindered by the coils around the rescuer's shoulders. These can be slipped over the head to leave the upper body free.

When the slot is prepared, a lark's foot or clove hitch is put around the axe at approximately two thirds of the way up the shaft towards the head (this is to provide an equal bearing surface to prevent the axe from pivoting). The axe is pushed horizontally into the head of the slot and the sling laid into the right-angle slot. A krab is clipped to the sling. A prussik loop is tied in an autobloc/French prussik around the tight rope as close as possible to the krab and then clipped to this. Now the prussik is pushed forward as tight as possible and the rescuer should slide forward gently to transfer the victim's weight to the autobloc (see Figure 3). The shoulder coils can be undone and removed methodically and finally then rope on the slack side of the autobloc should be clipped through the krab. This is now referred to as a *clutch*.

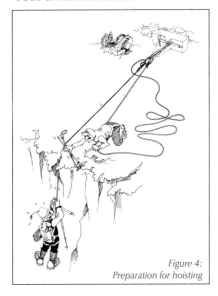

Figure 4:
Preparation for hoisting

For the rescuer to operate in safety he must be attached to the belay. The easiest way to do this is to attach himself temporarily to the belay with one prussik, then untie from the end of the rope and clip this to the belay. He should then attach himself to the rope via an Italian hitch into the screwgate krab on his harness. He must carefully approach the edge of the crevasse, paying out the rope through the hitch (effectively abseiling though not necessarily weighting the belay). Having ascertained that the victim needs pulling out, the edge of the crevasse must be prepared by pushing trekking poles under the rope as near to the edge as possible to prevent further cutting into the lip. The remaining snow lip can be broken away. The frightened victim must now be told to clip his ice axe and pole to his harness (see Figure 4).

If the rope hasn't bitten too far into the lip or the weight/strength difference of the walkers isn't to the rescuer's disadvantage, it should be possible to lift the victim using a 3:1 pulley system (sometimes referred to as a Z pulley). A second prussik loop is tied onto the taut rope close to the poles at the lip and a krab and pulley clipped to it. The slack rope from the clutch can now be clipped through the pulley. Pulling the rope back towards the belay now gives a mechanical advantage of 3:1. As the victim moves upwards the autobloc forming the clutch slackens and allows the rope to run through it. When the rescuer tires he can gently release the load and the clutch will reactivate and hold the victim's weight again. Similarly, when the pulley has been pulled up tight against the belay the clutch can be used to hold the victim whilst the pulley is slid back down the rope to start again (see Figure 5).

If the 3:1 doesn't work it can be quickly turned into a 6:1. The third prussik loop is tied onto the rope as it exits the pulley and the third krab is clipped to it. The other end of the rope – which up to now has protected the rescuer – can be

Figure 5: Hoist

Figure 6: Hoist

clipped through the third krab. Pulling on this results in a 6:1 system. The rescuer will have a fair amount of running around to do as for every 6m of rope he pulls in the victim will rise only 1m (see Figure 6).

Finally as the victim nears the lip he will have to try to extract the rope from where it has bitten in by pulling and bracing his feet against the wall of the crevasse. At the last moment the rescuer may be able to crawl forward to help the victim out.

NOTES

NOTES

THE GREAT OUTDOORS

tgo

FOR THE INDEPENDENT HILLWALKER AND BACKPACKER

THE GREAT OUTDOORS

tgo

Lakeland in Winter

Walking the Old County Tops

The UK's leading monthly magazine for the independent hillwalker and backpacker. With thought provoking articles, varied and exhilarating routes, expert gear reviews and outstanding photography, TGO's writers are at the heart of the walking world providing the essentials to inspire your next adventure.

To subscribe today call

0141 302 7718

Get ready for take off

Adventure Travel helps you to go outdoors over there

More ideas, information, advice and entertaining features on overseas trekking, walking and backpacking than any other magazine - guaranteed.

Available from good newsagents or by subscription - 6 issues £15

Adventure Travel Magazine T:01789-488166

LISTING OF CICERONE GUIDES